Higher Education Leadership
Analyzing the Gender Gap

Luba Chliwniak

ASHE-ERIC Higher Education Report Volume 25, Number 4

Prepared by

Clearinghouse on Higher Education
The George Washington University

In cooperation with

Association for the Study
of Higher Education

Published by

Graduate School of Education and Human Development
The George Washington University

Jonathan D. Fife, Series Editor

Cite as
Chliwniak, Luba. 1997. *Higher Education Leadership: Analyzing the Gender Gap.* ASHE-ERIC Higher Education Report Volume 25, No. 4. Washington, D.C.: The George Washington University, Graduate School of Education and Human Development.

Library of Congress Catalog Card Number 97-72902
ISSN 0884-0040
ISBN 1-878380-76-1

Managing Editor: Lynne J. Scott
Manuscript Editor: Alexandra Rockey
Cover Design by Michael David Brown, Inc., The Red Door
  Gallery, Rockport, ME

The ERIC Clearinghouse on Higher Education invites individuals to submit proposals for writing monographs for the *ASHE-ERIC Higher Education Report* series. Proposals must include:
1. A detailed manuscript proposal of not more than five pages.
2. A chapter-by-chapter outline.
3. A 75-word summary to be used by several review committees for the initial screening and rating of each proposal.
4. A vita and a writing sample.

ERIC **Clearinghouse on Higher Education**
Graduate School of Education and Human Development
The George Washington University
One Dupont Circle, Suite 630
Washington, DC 20036-1183

The mission of the ERIC system is to improve American education by increasing and facilitating the use of educational research and information on practice in the activities of learning, teaching, educational decision making, and research, wherever and whenever these activities take place.

This publication was prepared partially with funding from the Office of Educational Research and Improvement, U.S. Department of Education, under contract no. ED RI-88-062014. The opinions expressed in this report do not necessarily reflect the positions or policies of OERI or the Department.

EXECUTIVE SUMMARY

Where's the Gender Gap?

Only 16 percent of college and university presidents are women, only 13 percent of chief business officers are women, and only 25 percent of chief academic officers are women. Yet, more than 52 percent of the current student body comprises women. While colleges and universities are dominated by male leadership, however, concerns regarding administrative procedures that exclude women and create chilly campus climates continue to plague academic institutions. Many believe that by closing the leadership gap, institutions would become more centered on process and persons (described as feminized concerns) rather than focused on tasks and outcomes (attributed to masculine styles of leadership).

What Are the Issues of Institutional Context?

Most of us are intellectually aware of the complexity of women's situation and recognize that it needs to be viewed in a broad historical context of inclusion and exclusion. By exploring women's place in higher education institutions historically and currently, the lack of women's leadership is analyzed to determine the reasons for the gap and persistence factors in maintaining the gap.

Societal and organizational conceptions of leadership vary according to author assumptions. However, it is a common notion that leaders are individuals who provide vision and meaning for an institution and embody the ideals toward which the organization strives. Five common frames of reference for organizational structures inform us that leadership within these structures are traditionally conceived. Most conceptions of organizations assume that leadership emanates from the apex of a hierarchy. A sixth frame, A Web of Inclusion, is offered as an alternative, feminized frame of reference.

Women and Men Leaders: Different or Alike?

A problematic issue is that leadership traditionally has been studied using male norms as the standard for behaviors. As noted by Desjardins, Acker, Gutek, and others, women adopted male standards of success to better fit into male-dominated hierarchical structures and systems. Traditional scholars, such as Birnbaum and Mintzberg, view leaders as being alike and genderless. However, scholars such as

Barrie Thorne and Deborah Tannen, who research gender differences, posit that social norms and issues of gender-role ascription create differences between women and men.

Carol Gilligan's research on cognitive development has provided impetus for many of today's scholars to explore and revise leadership as we knew it. Gilligan argues that a single model of reasoning patterns and stages of moral development fails to capture the different realities of women's lives. By offering two different modes of reasoning patterns, a more complex but better understandable explanation for the human experience also would be more inclusive.

Sally Helgesen, for example, examines how women chief executive officers make decisions, gather and dispense information, delegate tasks, structure their organizations, and motivate their employees. She concludes that women leaders place more emphasis on relationships, sharing, and process, while male CEOs, as per Mintzberg's studies, focus on completing tasks, achieving goals, hoarding information, and winning. Gilligan's work identified a separate development pathway that results in personal and relational responsibility being of highest value for females and legalistic justice for individuals being highest for males. Therefore, as described by several authors, while men are more concerned with systems and rules, women are more concerned with relations and atmosphere.

Does the Gender Gap Matter?
Many authors have produced scholarship surrounding women's way of knowing compared with men's way of knowing. Recent scholarship speculates how these gender differences impact on the values held by leaders and how these values influence institutional structures and infrastructures. If styles and approaches are indistinguishable between women and men, the gender gap is a numerical inequity and should be corrected for ethical reasons. But, if leadership approaches are different, the gender gap may represent an impediment to potential institutional improvements.

The Glass Ceiling in Higher Education
Through intact male-dominated structures, men in organizations have come to view their perspectives and norms as being representative of gender-neutral human organizational structures and assume the structure is "asexual." Sheppard

found that these male filters render women's experiences as invisible. Subtle, indirect obstacles as a result of labeling or stereotyping place stumbling blocks in the career paths of many women. Cultural artifacts in higher education such as tenure-track standards, pedagogical practices, and marginalizing of certain studies and scholarship apparently preserve "appropriate" and different spheres for men and women in academe. A remedial vision — that is, one that is not seen through the eyes of only males — would add depth and new perspectives for shared images of posthierarchical institutional structures in higher education.

Implications to the Institution

Organizational culture affects curriculum and administration in that resources are allocated based on the values of the institution. Several scholars contend that a leader with an emerging, inclusive style of leadership could provide an institution with new values and ethics grounded in cooperation, community, and relationships within the community. Higher education's leadership also needs to become more reflective of the constituents it serves.

Several actions can be taken to bring about this change. Clearly, it is easier to promote change when in a position of authority. Transformational leadership develops organizational consensus and empowers those who are like-minded in their goals. Further, since patriarchy has been organized through men's relationships with other men, a similar unity among women is an effective means by which to combat institutionalized forms and norms that exclude women. And, regardless of position, women in higher education need to become more aware when the sense of being a marginal member or an unequal member of the academy impedes performance. A first step in this process is the elimination of campus micro-inequities, those behaviors and actions that create a chilly campus climate for women and minority groups.

It is important to remain vigilant to the effects of organizational norms, structures, and systems, for many of the issues encompassed within the gender gap are a result of systems and not individuals. However, because they are only systems, they can be examined and changed. Furthermore, of most importance in the process of change is the recognition that equality cannot be externally assigned until it has been internally perceived by institutional members. By attending to traditional institutional practices such as exclusionary tenure criteria, sexual harassment, and wage gaps, incremental but effective changes can reshape institutional culture and the associated images of leaders and leadership in higher education.

CONTENTS

Foreword   ix
Acknowledgments   xi

The Status of Women on Campuses and in Leadership Roles   1
Introduction   1
Background Issues   3
Presidential Profiles   6
Higher Education: Women's History Reviewed   9

Persistence Factors and Institutional Context   13
Introduction to the Persistence Factors   13
The Persistence Factors   14
Evaluations of Occupational Prestige   39
Summary of Persistence Factors   39

Gender Theory as a Form of Emerging Leadership Theory   43
Power and Leadership   43
Women's Leadership Style   44
Communication Patterns   49
Career Satisfaction   51
The Glass Ceiling   52

An Analysis of Leadership: Individual, Organizational, and Societal Conceptualizations   55
Introduction to Leadership Conceptualizations   55
What Is Leadership?   55
Societal Conceptualizations   56
The Relevance of Gender in Leadership Conceptualizations   59
Organizational Contexts   61
Individual Characteristics   65
Women's Leadership and the Leadership Frames   68
Summarizing Individual, Organizational, and Societal Conceptualizations   70

Factors Influencing Evaluations of Leaders and Leadership Modes   73
Evaluating Women as Leaders   73
Who Has the Right to Leadership Positions?   74
Summarizing Evaluations of Leaders   75

Conclusions, Implications, and Recommendations   77
Conclusions   77
Implications   79

Recommendations   80
A Final Note   85

References   **87**
Index   **99**
ASHE-ERIC Higher Education Reports   **117**
Advisory Board   119
Consulting Editors   121
Review Panel   123
Recent Titles   127
Order Form

FOREWORD

Research conference after research conference, policy conference after policy conference, during the last 20 years the findings have been the same:

- While there is a balance of women to men at the instructor and assistant professor level, there is a significant imbalance of men to women at the full professor, tenured level.
- Consistently at all levels, women receive lower salaries than men in all positions.
- At the upper leadership level — deans, vice presidents, and presidents — men are disproportionately represented to women.
- At institutions of higher reputational ranking, the disproportionate representation of men to women is even greater.

While these findings are well-known to most everyone in higher education, search committee after search committee still brings forth recommendations that perpetuate this gender discrimination. One reason is that the data are unclear. When search committees are asked about the lack of representation in their recommendations, the usual response is that there were no qualified women candidates. When the gender makeup of the usual search committee is analyzed, they more often are found to be highly male-dominated, thus leading to a suspicion of gender bias.

Hiring and promotion biases have been linked to compatibility. People generally recommend for promotion or for hiring those whom they like. Since people generally like only two types of people — those whom are like them or those whom they would like to be like — most promotional and hiring recommendations generally reflect the characteristics of the majority of a selection committee. What must happen to break this "compatibility cycle" is to increase a greater understanding and therefore a greater acceptance and respect for the gender difference.

In this report by Luba Chliwniak, who has served as campus director and director of education and compliance at Apollo College and now is a consultant on compliance programs for Pima Community College, the gender gap is carefully analyzed. After reviewing the current status of women in leadership positions, the author identifies and discusses the persistent factors related to the gender gap issues. She then heightens our awareness by turning from the conventional wisdom that underlies the persisting factors to examine research of gender theory as it relates to emerging theories of leadership. Dr. Chliwniak concludes her report with an analysis of the factors influencing evaluations of leaders and leadership modes and then presents conclusions and a series of recommendations for considerations for future hiring and promotion strategies.

This report of the gender issues related to higher education leadership helps to develop a greater understanding not only of what is the status of gender and leadership but why these gender inequities exist. This report, used as background for selection committees and by academic leaders who are in the position of nurturing and promoting women to positions of leadership responsibility, can only help to improve the gender climate in higher education.

Jonathan D. Fife
Series Editor,
Professor of Higher Education Administration, and
Director, ERIC Clearinghouse on Higher Education

AKNOWLEDGMENTS

My deepest gratitude is extended to Linda Munk, who initially read and edited this document for form, grammar, and content; to John Levin, who has helped me ponder and clarify gender-gap issues for two and one-half years; to Sheila Slaughter for her review, comments, and suggestions to improve this report; to Maxine Mott for her suggestions and guidance for improvement; to the ASHE-ERIC team of reviewers who provided valuable input into the content and flow of this product; and to Jonathan Fife, the series editor, who provided feedback, guidance, and encouragement in the preparation of this report. I could not have tackled such a project without these individuals and their assistance.

THE STATUS OF WOMEN ON CAMPUSES AND IN LEADERSHIP ROLES

Introduction

The student body in universities has changed significantly during the last several decades. Female enrollment of first-year students has matched and, in some coeducational institutions, surpassed male enrollment (Cage 1994). With the entering student body continuing to increase in female numbers, it might be assumed that the leadership of higher education institutions would reflect the demographics of the majority. This, in fact, has not been the case. The most recent data relating to the presidency and academic leadership in higher education institutions indicate that women are underrepresented in all leadership ranks. A gender gap continues to persist in this area of academe.

Many authors have produced scholarship surrounding the differences between women's ways of knowing compared to men's ways of knowing. Some write about differences as a result of deeply embedded social norms and expectations, referred to as the social construction of gender in our society. Others write from psychological or psychosocial perspectives, exploring how moral reasoning and social circumstances are different for men and women. Recent scholarship speculates how gender differences impact the values held by leaders in organizations and institutions and how these values influence institutional structures and infrastructures. It is a common notion, for example, that leaders provide the vision and the meaning for an institution and establish cultural values and norms. Further, the leader embodies the ideals of the institution and provides a direction for members. "In leadership, the situation of winning and losing is not important . . . leaders are concerned with management of people" and "inducing a group into action that is in accord with the shared purposes of all" (Bruhn 1993, p. 40). According to the literature, women's leadership style would create collegial, process-oriented environments in which fluid leadership offers empowerment to institutional members (Helgesen 1995, 1990; Auberdene and Naisbitt 1992; Kelly 1991). Men's leadership style, based on a traditional mode, implies a focus on structures, rules, outcomes, tasks, and hierarchy (Helgesen 1995, 1990; Johnson 1993; Milwid 1990).

When reviewing literature regarding leadership, whether within corporations or higher education, it can be readily discerned that current leadership theorists encourage a model that encompasses strong human-relations skills, a humanistic approach, collegiality, and consensus building (Levin 1994; Bergquist 1992; Wilcox and Ebbs 1992; Bennis 1991; Deegan, Tillery, and Associates 1991; Fryer 1991; Roueche, Baker, and Rose 1989). Tom Peters and Peter Drucker have made their preference for this model explicit in their current writings (Auburdene and Naisbitt 1992) as has Charles Garfield (1992). Another frame of reference, the web of inclusion (Helgesen 1995), emerges as a new posthierarchical model for organizations. Peters states that "the lumbering bureaucracies of this century will be replaced with fluid interdependent groups of problem solvers" (1994, p. 15) but warns that this can be accomplished only when a true posthierarchical organization is the result of cultural change. Senge's fifth discipline focuses on the development of learning organizations that are decentralized, nonhierarchical, and dedicated to the well-being and growth of employees (1990).

When cross-referencing postmodern, nonhierarchical leadership theories and models with gender-related research and scholarship, it becomes evident that the gender-related characteristics, described as innate to most women, encompass the very characteristics leadership theorists claim to be most effective.

This report explores women's place in higher education institutions historically and currently. Persistence factors, based on traditional policies and practices that define women as "other," establish sites of exclusion and inequity within the context of higher education institutions. It is within this context that the lack of women in leadership positions is analyzed to determine the reasons for the gender gap, the possible effects of the gap, and the potential impediment to institutional functioning if an emerging leadership style is not equally represented in academe.

This report deals with women in general. The lack of focus on race, ethnicity, and/or social class is recognized but the limited coverage does not preclude the need for future study. Previous studies have shown that most presidents self-identify as middle class, regardless of the social class of their family of birth. Also, women in general are underrepresented, therefore women of color and women from specific ethnic groups are very few in number. It is difficult to speak about minority women with this lack of research or evidentiary data for reference. For example, in 1990 male and female African-Americans represented only 5.5 percent of college presidents, and more than half of the African-American presidents headed historically black colleges or universities (Wilson 1995). Perhaps in the future as more women and minorities become involved in higher education leadership we can look forward to these issues of diversity being raised and researched with more representative numbers.

Only 16 percent of university and college presidents are women; yet women comprise over 52 percent of the student body.

Background Issues

Only 16 percent of university and college presidents are women; only 25 percent of academic deans are women; slightly over 18 percent of tenured full professors are women (*Women in Higher Education*, October 1995); yet women comprise over 52 percent of the student body (Cage 1994). While colleges and universities are dominated by traditional male leadership, concerns regarding administrative practices that exclude women and create chilly campus climates continue to be heard within academic institutions. These claims are made by members within and outside the academy.

A call to close the gender gap in leadership is spurred on by those who believe women's leadership would provide more equitable and caring environments for faculty, staff, and students in higher education (Wilcox and Ebbs 1992; Hensel 1991; Desjardins 1989; Wilkerson 1989). In closing the gender gap, institutions would become more centered on process and persons (described as emerging leadership concerns) rather than focused on tasks and outcomes (attributed to traditionally masculine styles of leadership). In turn, campus climates would be lived and viewed more positively by the current female majority of internal members.

In finding answers to the following questions, we will begin to determine the actual effect of the closing of the gender gap in leadership:

1. Are women leaders similar to men leaders in higher education institutions or is there diversity in leadership styles, values, and goals based on the gender of the leader?
2. Has academe tracked individuals and bypassed women for leadership positions based on old assumptions about the proclaimed natural affinity of males as leaders?

3. Are the leaders' values and goals reflected in the functioning of the institution?
4. Would women's leadership styles change the way higher education is conceived and organized?
5. Ultimately, would higher education be better if its conception and organization reflected the values of women leaders? If so, how?

Some of these questions will be difficult to answer because there are very few women leaders in higher education. Further, those who are in leadership positions often are found in small institutions (less than 3,000 students) and/or are in bureaucratic structures, often responding to a male chief executive officer, such as a district or system chancellor.

A relatively recent headline in the *Chronicle of Higher Education* tells us that "some top universities have a hard time finding a president (Sept. 15, 1995)." The article discusses how presidents are seduced into leaving their current institutions to accept positions with other institutions. The merry-go-round of presidents means that presidents serve an average of four to seven years in one institution. Unstated is the effectiveness of their leadership in the institutions they have led or the operational status of their current institution. The implication is clear, however, that these are desirable leaders. In each case, the presidential position is referred to in masculine terms, and in each case the named president was male. The lack of women in leadership positions and women as an available pool of candidates for presidential positions was not addressed in the article.

Flynn posits that boards may not be comfortable with selecting women for leadership roles because of a prevailing belief that men prefer to work with other men (1993). Reskin and Roos suggest that men, as a dominant group, have a stake in maintaining the differentiation of spheres (1990). Milwid (1990) and Kanter (1977) argue that the glass ceiling most often is the result of a woman being unlike her predecessor.

Aside from the obvious equity issue, the gender gap in leadership presents other problems related to its impact on higher education institutions. As the data show, women are underrepresented in every area of higher education leadership and, therefore, it is more difficult to study the actual impact of women's leadership on specific types of institutions with any significant numbers of women. This is especially the case for research universities in which only 7 percent of presidents are women (Ross, Green, and Henderson 1993).

Also problematic is that leadership traditionally has been studied using male norms in hierarchical structures as the standard for behaviors and characteristics against which women were assessed. Leaders were considered to be organizational and somewhat "asexual" rather than having distinctive gender-related modes and approaches (Sheppard 1992; Acker 1991; Gutek 1989). As a result, women adopted male standards of success to better fit into male-dominated, hierarchical organizational systems (Johnson 1993; Northcutt 1991; Desjardins 1989). Students also see and feel the lack of a feminized leadership style. With more than half of the student body being women (Cage 1994), it is difficult for women to understand how a system that is not based on diversity will change dramatically enough or rapidly enough to provide environments that are suitable and welcoming for all its students without a larger representation of women in the leadership ranks (Pearson et al. 1989).

In summary, the background issues relating to the gender gap are most pronounced in the disparity between numbers of women leaders (16 percent of higher education leaders [Rigaux 1995]) in relationship to the numbers of women who earn advanced degrees (44 percent of doctorates [Finkel and Olswang 1995]), the number of women professors (25 percent), and female full professors (18 percent) in universities (Finkel and Olswang 1995). A call to close the gender gap is spurred on by those who believe that participatory styles of leadership will help to alleviate concerns regarding institutional exclusionary practices, chilly campus climates, and masculinized priorities. If leadership styles are different between men and women — that is, if women are more likely to provide participatory environments — then the gender gap may represent an impediment to potential institutional improvements. But if styles and approaches are the same, the gender gap then would appear to be an issue of inequity based on outdated assumptions and perceptions rather than actual differences. The current selection process, particularly in the case of boards who seduce seated male presidents to relocate for their institution's leadership, indicate that gender is salient only in terms of who is not selected rather than who is selected.

Leadership traditionally has been studied using male norms, or the generic man, as the standard by which females were assessed. Although leadership in the abstract is gender-neutral, current scholars speculate that there are distinctive gender-related modes and approaches to leadership. Although women attempted to adopt male behaviors to better fit into male-dominated systems, the data indicate that the tactic appears to have been somewhat less than successful (e.g. Johnson 1993; Eagly, Makhijani, and Klonsky 1992; Eagly and Karau 1991; Kelly 1991) as women continue to be underrepresented in every area of higher education leadership.

Presidential Profiles
The most current data on women in higher education presidential positions are provided through a study conducted by the American Council on Education, Office of Women in Higher Education, as reported by Rigaux (1995). The data indicate that of 2,903 higher education institutions, branch and affiliated campuses, 16 percent are headed by women presidents. A 4 percent increase in women presidents occurred between 1992 data and 1995 data. Further, Rigaux reports that the highest proportion of women leaders are found in private two-year institutions (27 percent) and women are more likely to lead small institutions, with 71 percent of female leaders at colleges and universities with full-time enrollments of less than 3,000 students (Rigaux 1995). Twenty-two percent of institutions with 3,000 to 10,000 students are led by women and, unchanged from 1992, only 7 percent of institutions with more than 10,000 students are led by women (Rigaux 1995).

A "snapshot" of a university or college president in 1990 is provided in *The American College President: A 1993 Edition* (Ross, Green, and Henderson 1993). Surveys were administered by the American Council on Education from 1986 through 1990. Of the 2,423 respondents, 287 were women (11.8 percent) and 2,136 were men (88.2 percent). The number of women showed improvement over the 1986 "snapshot" when only 9.5 percent of presidents were women. The results of the survey indicated that in 1990, women, in comparison with men, were more likely to: be single (51 percent vs. 9 percent); if married, have an employed spouse (86 percent vs. 48 percent); and be working at an independent baccalaureate institution (29 percent vs. 18 percent) or an independent two-year institution (10 percent vs. 5 percent). Of the newly appointed women during this period, 44 percent received appointments in two-year colleges. "Traditionally, women's colleges have afforded women the greatest opportunities to attain presidencies. As leadership positions in coeducational institutions have gradually opened to women, the percentage of women presidents who head women's colleges has decreased" (Ross, Green, and Henderson 1993, p. 20).

Noticeable differences exist among types of institutions and the numbers of women who head these particular types. This data finding provides further evidence that "there are distinct institutional identities, traditions and cultures" (Ross, Green, and Henderson 1993, p. 20). Table 1 categorizes four types of institutions and the corresponding number of women presidents in each category as reported by Rigaux (1995) with data from the American Council on Education, Office of Women in Higher Education.

TABLE 1

INSTITUTIONAL TYPE	# WOMEN PRESIDENTS	% WOMEN PRESIDENTS
PRIVATE	237	
Private, 4-year	199	15%
Private, 2-year	38	27%
PUBLIC	216	
Public, 4-year	78	14%
Public, 2-year	138	9%
Total women presidents	453	16%
Total U.S. institutions	2,903	16%

Source: The American Council on Education, Office of Women in Higher Education, as reported by Rigaux (1995) in The Community College Week.

Even though there have been increases in numbers of women presidents since 1990, when women accounted for only 12 percent of higher education presidents (Ross, Green, and Henderson 1993), as the data in Table 1 indicate, the public sector has an even larger gender gap in leadership than the independent higher education system. The results of a 1990 presidential profile showed that most presidents come to their position from the same type of institution they are leading (Ross, Green, and Henderson 1993). This is especially true for community colleges, where 75 percent of presidents held a prior position within a community college. Of further interest is that of all university and college presidents, more than one-quarter were internal candidates, and most had held a position as a vice president or chief academic officer (Ross, Green, and Henderson 1993).

Ross, Green, and Henderson provide us with insight into the future of women in higher education leadership based on their 1990 findings (1993). Assuming that all of the same conditions that were in place from 1986 through 1990 continue without change, they forecast that women will achieve the same percentage of presidencies as their percentage of the general population (about half of the population) in approximately 50 years — the year 2040. This time frame would seem to be unacceptable if equity and equality are issues in leadership. It would seem critical to more quickly include the values and talents of persons now being overlooked for higher education leadership positions due to their gender.

With a Professional Experience Profile, Morgan and Clark examine five factors that influence attainment of presidential positions for women college and university presidents (1995). Of 169 respondents, 74 percent rated professional experience as having the greatest influence, while mentoring was rated by only 4 percent of the subjects as influencing attainment (Morgan and Clark 1995). The majority of respondents either were recruited or nominated into their positions. Half of the respondents rated educational background as having the second greatest influence in attaining the presidency and did not believe that networking had been helpful in securing these positions.

Currently, most women leaders at the presidential level are found in community and junior colleges and particularly in colleges with less than 3,000 students. Furthermore, the independent sector in higher education has provided the most opportunity for women leaders at the presidential level. Although these data indicate differences by institutional type, a comparative analysis that includes recruitment process, selection-committee membership, and final-selection authority may provide the type of information needed to determine why this phenomenon exists. It could be inferred, however, that the less formal and bureaucratic the institution, the higher the probability that a woman will succeed in being selected.

Higher Education: Women's History Reviewed

From a historical perspective, monitoring the progress of women as students, faculty, and leaders provides us with insight into the current status of women in universities and colleges. Most of us are intellectually aware of the complexity of women's situation and recognize that it needs to be viewed in a broad historical context of institutional inclusion and exclusion. To better understand the context and status of women in higher education institutions, a brief historical perspective is included for review.

The first institution of higher education in the United States was Harvard College, founded in 1636. In the 17th century, the belief commonly was held that women were intellectually inferior to men. Women were expected to remain in the domestic sphere, whereas education was reserved for the cultured gentlemen. "Higher Education for most women was obtainable only in women's academies which were little more, and frequently less, than finishing schools" (Brookover 1965, p. 6). There was a concern that women either would become infertile and/or strong-minded through the rigors of education. Further, a lack of attentiveness to men's academic obligations could occur if surrounded by women in coeducational institutions (Miller-Solomon 1985; Brookover 1965).

In the 1820s common schools were opened, in part, to help close the illiteracy gap between men and women. By 1850, more than half of the women in the United States could read and write (Bengiveno 1995). However, women's education was viewed only for its importance in relationship to men. Educated women were needed to raise the next generation of young men into statesmen and philosophers and to be agreeable companions for their well-placed husbands (Bengiveno 1995; Miller-Solomon 1985; Ferguson 1984). In essence, education was perceived as a vehicle for making women better wives, homemakers, and mothers.

Many events and evolutions brought change to the education and employment of women. One such event was the passage of legislation that helped to open academe's doors to women. "In 1862 Lincoln's signing of the Morrill Land Grant Act affirmed the importance of public higher education . . . although the legislation had not specifically referred to women, as old institutions were enlarged and new ones created, women gradually established their right to attend . . ." (Miller-Solomon 1985, p. 44).

The first eight state universities to accept women were Iowa (1855); Wisconsin (1867); Kansas, Indiana, and Minnesota (1869); and Missouri, Michigan, and California (1870) (Miller-Solomon 1985). Cornell provided the lead for private universities by giving equal status to women and men in 1872 (Smith 1990). Some universities made arrangements to teach women, but these arrangements usually were carried out in annexed institutions or coordinate colleges. The refusal of some schools to provide equal access for women contributed to the creation of normal schools for women (Miller-Solomon 1985). Although many state universities were coeducational, women's colleges were considered to be superior institutions for women. Some female colleges, modeled after male institutions, came to represent strong academic institutions. These colleges were Vassar (1865), Wellesley (1870), Smith (1871), Bryn Mawr (1885), and Mount Holyoke (1888) (Bengiveno 1995).

Between 1870 and 1900, the number of women enrolled in higher education institutions increased by almost 800 percent. Although many more women were entering colleges and universities, the female faculty at women's schools presented limited role models for their students due to the limitation of only single women having access to academic posts at women's colleges (Miller-Solomon 1985). Public universities also often did not offer an alternative model of a married, female professor. Although female students significantly were increasing in numbers, "the census of 1890 listed 7,358 men and 4,194 women faculty . . . by 1910 there were 19,151 men as opposed to 4,717 women faculty" (Smith 1990, p. 67). Male faculty had increased by two and one-half times to accommodate the growth in higher education, but women had increased by a mere 500 — approximately 10.5 percent. Although by 1940 women accounted for 28 percent of faculty, this number was not reached again until the beginning of the 1990s (Miller-Solomon 1985).

In 1920, women's enrollment in higher education peaked at slightly over 47 percent and by the 1930s, approximately 15 percent of Ph.D.s were awarded to women. Women tended to gravitate to those traditionally feminized areas in which there was apparent comfort and acceptance. Psychology, sociology, economics, and applied chemistry in home economics were the dominant fields for women in the academic world (Miller-Solomon 1985). Education soon followed as a field highly dominated by women. But an unmistakable division existed between marriage and paid employment. Combining marriage and career was an alternative path only for women with a pioneering spirit (Miller-Solomon 1985). Additionally, prejudices toward the employment and advancement of married women not only limited professional opportunities but also discouraged the pursuit of professions with long-term training requirements.

Although World War II brought women more fully into academe and the workforce, the peacetime that followed brought setbacks. With returning veterans, the social acceptance of male priority caused women to lose the many strides they had gained in showing their diverse talents in academic pursuits as well as versatility in employment. For example, during the 1930s and 1940s, women accounted for 40 percent or more of undergraduate students. By 1950, this number dipped to 31 percent, and it was not until 1970 that women's participation rate in undergraduate studies returned to a level of 40 percent. "Thus, in the 1970s women of several generations initiated demands for female equality and challenged educational institutions to fulfill the promises of liberal education" (Miller-Solomon 1985, p. 188) and so too began challenges to the single-gender, linear view of society (Kuk 1990).

But also during the 1970s most parents still expected their daughters to become wives and mothers. Parents felt torn between pride in their daughters' achievements and worry about the possible sacrifice of a family in favor of a job (Milwid 1990). Critics of the women's movement longed for the nostalgic prefeminist bliss where women provided safe and nurturing havens and devotion to family, hearth, and home (Faludi 1991; Ferguson 1984).

It is with this brief historical perspective that we arrive at the 1990s and the continuing conversation about women's place in higher education institutions and society.

PERSISTENCE FACTORS AND INSTITUTIONAL CONTEXT

Introduction to the Persistence Factors

Whether one examines curriculum, student norms, classroom norms, permanent faculty appointments, or higher education leadership, there is compelling evidence that the different voice of women is not yet fully included in institutional culture. The academy has comfortably reproduced itself for several centuries and a male-dominated, patriarchal culture has been solidly established. Many patterns of sex and gender relations in contemporary society "go unnoticed because they are so deeply embedded in the minds of women and men that, unless they become a problem, we take these patterns of everyday life for granted . . ." (Anderson 1988, p. 3). It is in this context that women as students, faculty, and staff attempt to change institutional patterns and garner acceptance as institutional leaders.

Organizational culture affects curriculum, faculty, and administration in that resources are allocated based on the values of the institution (Kuh et al. 1991; Mintzberg 1989; Masland 1985). Four key components of a strong culture include values, heroes, rites and rituals, and a cultural network — a communication system through which cultural values are instituted and reinforced. "A point of agreement among most organizational-culture scholars is the notion that cultures are socially created through the interaction of organizational actors" (Miller 1995, p. 112) and this needs to shift due to environmental changes. Millett refers to this phenomenon as "interior colonization" of society and organizations (1990).

The effect of patriarchal leadership (leadership that is male-dominated and normed on male standards) often results in masculine norms perpetuated throughout the institutional structure and culture. Faculty ranks, tenured full professorships, and the production and presentation of scholarship continue to present the "generic man" as being the norm while women's location is marginalized or even excluded (Gumport 1991, 1988). As a result, students receive patterns of information that perpetuate the continuation of the status quo, namely the generic male model in a male-dominated institution. Women, on the other hand, continue to hover on the fringe of the institution regardless of equal numbers to men (Kuk 1990). Images of leadership are based on stereotypic masculine traits and characteristics (Blackmore 1993; Kelly 1991; Northcutt 1991; Milwid

1990; Desjardins 1989; Burton 1987), and women have not been successful in adopting these traits. In most cases women who exhibit male characteristics are downgraded for such attempts. Administrative leadership has come to be associated with an image of a rational, logical, objective, and aggressive male (Blackmore 1993; Sheppard 1992; Desjardins 1989; Burton 1987). An acceptance of emerging and diverse leadership models that include the strengths of both genders needs support and exploration to dispel myths of the generic man as the ideal. Challenges to existing institutional norms and patterns of socialization need to be pursued so that an integration of new thought and changing values and practices can be established in higher education institutions.

The Persistence Factors

The causes for the perpetuation of the gender gap are many. Each persistence factor can be studied independently to gain a perspective of the impact on the gender gap in higher education. When combined, however, these institutional persistence factors seem like insurmountable barriers for some women. Women continue to meet more challenges and barriers than men who seek leadership positions. Historically and currently, women in academe challenge social, personal, and professional perspectives that impede their full acceptance as members of the academy. Women chief executive officers in higher education who attained presidential positions are proof, however, that the challenge for attainment can be met.

The eight persistence factors in the perpetuation of higher education's gender gap include the following.

Affirmative action/reaction

Although there seemed to be some understanding and appreciation for the intent of affirmative action and equal-employment opportunity regulations and guidelines when established, as time moved forward the citizenry began to lose clarity of its intent. Perhaps it was through misinformation or perceived experiences, but affirmative-action plans began to be regarded not as corrective devices for classes of people who historically had been treated differently from others but as reasons for reverse discrimination, particularly of white males as a group (Aufderheid 1992).

Feminists do not question whether AA/EEO is a failure; they do, however, question why a good notion became a national problem. They contend that the affirmative-action programs implemented and maintained during the Carter administration lost ground during President Reagan's administration (Faludi 1991; Washington and Harvey 1989). Reagan's backsliding and "no problem" attitude regarding the effects of downsizing federal monitoring offices (including the Department of Education's Women's Educational Equity Act program) caused affirmative-action intent to become "only words without power against discriminatory practices" (Faludi 1991, p. 363). Some argue that the Reagan administration reinstated discourse emphasizing the white male head of the family model, and discussions of equality were replaced with rhetoric of "hierarchy of difference" based on economic need (Kelly 1991). Gloria Steinem contends that the Bush administration carried forward the Reagan administration rhetoric regarding male privilege in a family model (1994).

Critical approaches to understanding organizational culture have philosophical roots in the work of Karl Marx. This approach has been instrumental in shaping the work of theorists and scholars who take a "critical" perspective in social research. One role of the critical theorist is to explore and uncover imbalances in power and make them known to oppressed groups (Miller 1995). Critical race theory provides a perspective on the affirmative-action dilemma. Those concerned with ethnic and race issues find the problem is surrounded by legal parameters. "The failure of affirmative-action programs rests with a fundamental question of who 'owns' the problem: The institution or the structure that creates and perpetuates inequality, or the affected individual or group" (Washington and Harvey 1989, p. 11)? Although the issue of affirmative action is more complex than one institution and one individual, the magnitude of the problem is amplified when considering there are approximately 3,000 higher education institutions in the United States.

It is argued that institutional conditions favorable to affirmative action require strong support from institutional leadership and that a core of women and minorities within the institution need to be given authority to monitor progress. Leaders who have been successful in setting institutional agendas regarding affirmative action are identified by their influence on institutional action through "personal commitment, attention to the issue, and effective use of incentives" (Hanna 1988, p. 374). Hanna's study as well as her review of previously conducted studies in the area of affirmative action show that the ability of a leader to set an institutional agenda is one of the most powerful tools utilized to shape the values of an institution. From a critical perspective, one then would need to ask: Who are the leaders currently shaping the values of institutions? Who wins and who loses in this process? Who has the power to change the leadership?

During the 1990s, a heated debate emerged among the public at large and national legislators regarding the continuation and/or demise of affirmative action as a legal tool for achieving equity. Women's reactions are mixed. *Working Woman* magazine (July 1995) compared a March 1995 poll sponsored by *Newsweek* and a March 1995 poll sponsored by *NBC News/Wall Street Journal* on government involvement and the fairness of hiring preferences with affirmative-action programs. Overall, the polls indicated a fairly even split among women about whether affirmative-action programs should continue. Only among nonwhite women was there overwhelming support for affirmative action — about three-quarters of those surveyed favored it for women and blacks.

Although white women have benefited from the affirmative-action movement, they apparently do not see themselves as great beneficiaries (Alpern 1995). Interestingly, the greatest predictors of public opinion regarding affirmative action are party affiliation (Republican women favored dismantling affirmative action) and race (African-Americans supported affirmative action), according to the Princeton Survey Research group, which conducted the poll on behalf of *Newsweek* (Alpern 1995). According to the poll, if affirmative action simply were eliminated, less than a quarter of all the women surveyed believed the status of working women would deteriorate, whereas slightly more than half of the women predicted women's status would remain the same (Alpern 1995). It is speculative whether these data capture women's views of affirmative-action policies or whether the data represent women's pessimism regarding the effect of implementation and enforcement of current affirmative-action policies and programs.

In higher education, for example, according to Hanna's study of affirmative-action policies for faculty women, habit and tradition regulate committee activities and selections (1988). "To a large extent, familiarity unconsciously colored the evaluations of candidates in the hiring process . . . applicants from prestige institutions who had worked with colleagues of search committee members tended to be viewed more positively than other applicants" (Hanna 1988, p. 379). Wilson suggests one reason for the lack of African-American women in higher education leadership positions is the "double whammy" — that is, belonging to two groups facing discrimination (1995). The term coined for the artificial barriers to advance African-Americans is the "concrete wall." For females, it is the "glass ceiling."

In July 1995, Gov. Pete Wilson of California successfully spearheaded a campaign to abolish affirmative-action policies for the California State University System. The board of regents agreed with his position and lifted affirmative-action policies for one of the largest higher education systems in the United States. The state of Texas followed in 1996, eliminating racial preferences for admissions into the state's higher education institutions. The ramifications of these actions only can be speculated upon at this time, but Wilson claims this to be a victory for the "angry white male" whom, he states, has been experiencing reverse discrimination for almost 30 years through the active recruitment and hiring of minorities and women while affirmative-action policies have been in place. Derrick Bell states, "Affirmative-action programs are now caught in a morass of opposition and uncertainty similar to that engendered by school-desegregation programs" (1997). He believes that advocates of affirmative action and equal-employment opportunity "must devise new approaches to achieve and maintain diversity in student bodies, faculties, and administrative ranks" to insulate diversity programs from attacks which eliminate racial and gender classifications.

Affirmative action has come to be perceived not as establishment of corrective action plans but as the reason for reverse discrimination. However, the leader who sets an institutional agenda to shape values in favor of diversity and the leader who espouses a personal commitment to the issue can help regulate the habits and traditions of those who unconsciously follow a traditional — often self-reproducing — path in the candidate-selection processes.

The affirmative-action issue is complex, and while this report briefly skims the various perspectives involved in the issue, questions remain regarding the impact of affirmative action on leadership ranks in higher education. In particular, it is unclear whether the strides women have made in obtaining presidential, dean, or faculty positions during the last 10 years will be curtailed without the legal oversight encompassed within affirmative-action policies. And, if history is our teacher in this matter, it appears that affirmative-action programs should not be abolished until the need for such programs also is abolished; that is, when equity is achieved.

Curriculum and scholarship: the perpetuation of the gap

Leadership theories and models promoted in colleges and universities too often are not scrutinized closely enough to assure that there is comparable imaging of male and female positions, perspectives, and power. Although current authors concern themselves with gender-neutral references in their texts, there often is a forgotten second concern — that of the underpinnings of the work. Images are being conceived in response to those unwritten but perceived nuances. Anderson posits that the absence or invisibility of women in the ivory tower contributes to the detachment of reality and distortion of women in the curriculum (1988). "Moreover, persons who participate in the life of an institution tend to share its definitions of reality . . ." thereby perpetuating old notions in new writings (Anderson 1988, p. 36).

Until efforts at transforming the curriculum started taking shape, the traditionally accepted purpose of higher education was to educate young white males. Even though women comprise the majority of the student body, they still are considered to be a minority group on the fringe of institutional norms (Kuk 1990). As a result, much of the leadership research and literature continues to concern itself with the male experience and therefore perpetuates the assumption of a patriarchal model. There is a lack of gender balance both in context and content. "It is ironic that women students themselves may unwittingly collude in its perpetuation. When no representation of women's experience appears in the curriculum, a woman student is encouraged to believe the 'generic man' includes her" (Schuster 1985, p. 18).

Allan Bloom in *The Closing of the American Mind* (1987) espoused the notion that "the latest enemy of the vitality of the classic text is feminism" (in Faludi 1991, p. 290). This protection of the Western classics does not provide for the plurality evidenced on the campuses in America. Nor does this protectionism combat the concept that these classic texts are contributing to the patriarchal images that have continued to plague those who are attempting to bring a more equal definition of humanity onto the curriculum. Bloom takes feminists to task in that he believes "the souls of men . . . must be dismantled" if the classics are not maintained in their pure form (in Faludi 1991, p. 295). His stance is representative of other scholars who are debating the status of the curriculum and its reconstruction.

> *Two recent postmodernist movements, constructivism and deconstruction, challenge the idea of a single meaning of reality and concern themselves with the way meaning is represented. The current interest in constructivism and deconstruction is part of a widespread skepticism about the positivist tradition in science and essentialist theories of truth and meaning* (Hare-Mustin and Marecek 1988, p. 455).

The construction of gender, the result of deeply embedded social norms and expectations and their deconstruction, the ferreting-out of certain meanings and interpretations within texts, show how discourse can reveal alternative meanings and reveal how reality is invented through representative meanings derived from language, history, and culture. "Thus, whereas positivism [founded in historically accepted belief systems] asks what are the facts, constructivism asks what are the assumptions; whereas positivism asks what are the answers, constructivism asks what are the questions" (Hare-Mustin and Marecek 1988, p. 456).

Traditionalists as positivists and feminist scholars as constructionists and deconstructionists debate the representation of reality in the canon and traditional curriculum (Haworth and Conrad 1990). The tension between traditional and emerging scholarship creates a dilemma for the academy in that current curriculum norms need to be broken down and reconstructed with multiple views and different voices to enable emerging curriculum to become fully integrated into academe. Others believe that this very effort would dilute truth in knowledge (for example, Trow, D'Souza, Bloom, and Hirsch).

In reaction to deconstructionism, an accreditor that recognizes traditional liberal arts colleges, the American Academy of Liberal Education, or AALE, was established in 1992. In support of this new group, the National Association of Scholars, "a group that has opposed the national movement to make the college curriculum more multicultural" (Wilson 1997), helped secure a $100,000 grant to start the academy. The academy's 16 educational standards include "the study of political, philosophical, and cultural history of Western Civilization."

Thomas Aquinas College, accredited by AALE, for example, has implemented a "great books" curriculum whereby all students follow the same required course schedule and declare no academic major. In reaction to the Rhodes College president seeking AALE accreditation, an anonymous Rhodes professor stated, "We don't want to be identified as an institution that is no longer open-minded, tolerant, and progressive" (Wilson 1997). The president of the college refers to these types of reaction from faculty as "just a good healthy difference of opinion." The faculty, however, wonder whether the academy promotes rigor or curbs diversity. To date, AALE has accredited Thomas Aquinas College and the University of Dallas. It is considering applications from Baylor University and James Madison College. Rhodes College is the only institution in which faculty members opposed the accreditation process and standards.

Social and ethical issues that result from either naive approaches to research or cowardice on the part of the researcher are found in social research and scientific studies (Scarr 1988). Without including gender and minority differences in research efforts, the variables that inform us as to how underrepresented populations best can be served will continue to be elusive. But the questions asked in these research efforts also can become problematic.

If questions about minorities and women are framed in terms of what is wrong with, deficient about, or needs improvement for these underrepresented groups, then the research outcomes for such groups are very likely to be negative. If the standard for good behavior is always the white male group, then the behavior of women and ethnic minorities is likely to seem negative (Scarr 1988, p. 57).

Until recently, scholarship on leadership continued to use the white male as the exemplar of leadership style and characteristics. The context of these studies also were prone to bias toward women and minorities. Due to the nature of organizational context, these studies often were conducted in organizations that were male-dominated and hierarchical in nature. Within the last 10 years, feminists and other emergent scholars such as Helgesen, Peters, Bennis, Nanus, and Covey have challenged these dominant norms with questions about traditional assumptions from constructionist and deconstructionist perspectives. Women began their own research efforts to determine if actual differences based on gender existed or if there were deficiencies in prior research methodology. Gilligan's research on women's moral development was spurred by a recognition that categories of knowledge are human constructions and the recognition of how accustomed we have become to seeing life through men's eyes (1982). In such a context, woman has appeared to be the deviant model while the male model is the norm. Carolyn Desjardins (1989) and Sally Helgesen (1995 and 1990), as two examples of feminized leadership scholars, offer alternative models of leadership based on gender-related theory. These feminist perspectives are in addition to emerging leadership theory, which will be discussed later in this report.

Traditional notions of leadership continue to be perpetuated in colleges and universities through curriculum and scholarship produced by those who share a common definition of reality. Although much of the leadership research and literature concerns itself with the male experience, recent movements in theory development challenge existing notions of reality based on traditional beliefs and assumptions. The white male as the exemplar of leadership characteristics and leadership styles leaves women and minorities in the position of being negatively evaluated, and even appearing deviant, against these norms. Yet, efforts to revisit a seemingly biased curriculum has caused tension between traditional scholars and postmodern or emergent scholars in the academy. While one group views their work to be

Until recently, scholarship on leadership continued to use the white male as the exemplar of leadership style and characteristics.

based on empirical research and hard facts, the other group claims these facts do not include women and minority subjects equally nor do they refer to inclusionary organizational systems. Postmodern theorists argue that since the mid-1960s we have been living in a different world and that a new kind of understanding is required for this postindustrial and global society (Miller 1995). One postmodern notion, for example, is that we no longer can rely on looking for universals and essentials in knowledge; rather, "knowledge can best be constituted in 'micro-narratives' that encompass the fragmented and constantly changing nature of today's society" (Miller 1995, p. 139).

Women faculty and tenure

Although the status and representation of women in academe has improved since the 1960s resurgence of the women's movement, female faculty remain underrepresented on most campuses. Several recent studies found that women comprised about one-fourth of the faculty but only about one-10th of the tenured, full professors (Hensel 1991). Hensel determines the probable time line for equal representation in all areas of academe and states that "at the current rate of increase, it will take women 90 years to achieve equal representation to men on American campuses" (1991, p. 11). However, a survey conducted by the American Council on Education indicated the number of full professors rose to 18 percent, showing evidence of progress in women's representation (Rigaux 1995).

These data are significant not only because of the leadership gap (in a university setting, tenure being a strong predictor for chief academic officer and presidential positions), but also because of the scholarship being produced. When men continue to dominate the faculty ranks, so too is the production and publication of scholarship. Equally disturbing is the lack of professional role models from whom junior female faculty can seek counseling and guidance on issues such as institutional culture, grant writing, publishing standards, committee memberships, and the like. Women then turn to male role models to define their professional success, even though personal definitions of success have been shown to be different between women and men.

The lack of diversity in the makeup of tenured professors in the majority of four-year and doctoral-level institutions creates a perpetual cycle of repeating established institutional norms. Institutional culture of academe has supported a social matrix that delineates roles, expectations, and aspirations for its members by structuring barriers for some and opening doors for others.

Townsend speculates that two-year institutions may have less-sexist environments because the tenure process usually is based on length of service (1995). She finds that in most cases an instructor receives tenure after three consecutive years of service and, if there is a hierarchical ranking, it usually is related to the attainment of a doctorate as well as additional years of service.

The attainment of tenure has been elusive for many women faculty in university environments. Tenure tracks continue to be reserved for male faculty, while females occasionally slip in through small cracks that have formed in educational institutions. But, when the number of tenured women faculty reaches 12 percent, other women faculty are more likely to be granted tenure (Hensel 1991). This critical mass of 12 percent provides for representation within power centers not accessible to those in lower ranks or positions. Access makes possible the vocalization necessary to combat gender-biased judgments in tenure decisions with the most important factor being the production of scholarship (Phillip 1993). Gumport argues that while a critical mass of like-minded colleagues is sufficient for establishing an academic niche, it may not be sufficient for subsequent institutionalization unless some control over criteria for evaluating scholarship is gained (1991).

Another important element potentially combated by the 12 percent critical mass is shown by a 1992 meta-analysis of gender and evaluation of leaders by Eagly, Makhijani, and Klonsky. The researchers conclude that women should avoid roles and situations in which men serve as evaluators (although admittedly difficult to do, based on the numbers). Men tend to devaluate women's contributions as being less noteworthy. This issue is critical in that this selection devaluation phenomenon serves to preserve the traditional division of labor and discourage women from seeking positions that offer higher income and status (Eagly, Makhijani, and Klonsky 1992).

Slaughter's research on retrenchment in the 1980s shows another disturbing fact regarding women's tenure (1993).

During periods of retrenchment, centrality to the university mission was not considered as critical as other external economic factors. Slaughter found that women faculty, positioned in disciplines in which high minority and female enrollments exist (such as education and the humanities), were retrenched at higher rates than other more highly male-dominated disciplines such as the sciences and engineering. Remaining faculty were expected to maintain higher student and course loads to make up for lost faculty even though numbers of students were not reduced. Faculty members also were expected to continue publishing and providing community service outside of their extended responsibilities, whereas faculty in male-dominated disciplines continued to maintain smaller course and student loads and were able to include research and community service time within their dedicated institutional time.

Studies from the field of social psychology continue to document differences between men and women in attribution theories. Women internalize their failures and externalize their successes, whereas the opposite is true for men (Bengiveno 1995). Such beliefs can be detrimental to women in their professional advancement, particularly in an academic career. Where women view rejection of a book or article as personal and often put the work away, men externalize the reasons for the rejection and resubmit the work elsewhere for review. These studies indicate that the rules of the game, which includes publishing for gaining tenure, are played differently by the academician depending upon the gender of the player. It can be inferred from these studies that professional wisdom calls for resubmitting work, regardless of quality, to attain quantity for tenure decisions. Attribution theory, perhaps, can give some insight into issues to be addressed when tenure procedures call for productivity, and male committee members define productivity as quantity and not necessarily quality.

Astin and Davis conducted a study of women's academic careers and publication (1985). Of special interest is the finding that "married women's careers resembled those of men more closely than did the professional careers of single women" (p. 416). Further, "Single women are much more likely than married men or women to be involved with research and teaching at minority research and studies centers, including women's studies centers" (Astin and Davis 1985, p.

419). Married women become involved in these activities later, after becoming more established. The researchers also found that working in centers rather than having a home department impedes tenure, salary, and promotion decisions since centers — particularly women's-studies centers — historically have been viewed as being marginal in academe.

Another important finding in the study is that single women have the highest rate of published books over their careers. Astin and Davis suggest, however, that single women would be wiser to publish articles rather than books at the beginning stages of an academic career to more closely fit the established tenure model.

Tenure is a strong predictor for positions as chief academic officers, and most presidents in higher education have held the post of chief academic officer. However, only 18 percent of full professors in universities are women (*Women in Higher Education*, October 1995). Although this appears to indicate that a critical mass of women in faculty ranks has been reached, it may not be sufficient for institutionalization of revised cultural norms. Conversely, as 82 percent of full professors are male, there still is inequitable control over criteria for evaluating scholarship or scholars. A selective devaluation phenomenon persists even though productivity for female faculty is indicative of being equal but different from productivity for male faculty members.

Women's studies and feminist scholarship

"The first wave of women's studies courses brought women as a group (rather than isolated individuals) onto the syllabus, yet their most striking characteristic was their oppression" (Schuster 1985, p. 22). Rather than celebrating the dual experience of being women and being part of humanity, the focus was on the downtrodden female. This powerful imaging concept did not necessarily enhance the status of women in the academy or women's leadership. Even though women's studies have taken many forms in the curriculum and in the institution, there continues to be a perspective that it does not shape relations among men and women academics in the academy.

The marginalized location of women's-studies programs in institutions projects an image that is not comparable to the broader composition of academic departments and disciplines. By their location in the academy, fields such as women's studies are grounded in definitions of difference. Difference implies resistance to attempts at incorporation and appropriation of curriculum (Thompson and Tyagi 1993). This location, originally thought to be a place where the voices of women could be heard, became perceived as a place where "women libbers" espouse theories that were contrary to inclusion in the so-called normal curriculum. "The point is not simply that one should have a voice; the more crucial question concerns the sort of voice one comes to have as a result of one's location both as an individual and as part of a collective" (p. 61).

Feminist scholarship refers to "a system of values that challenges male dominance and advocates social, political, and economic equity of women and men in society" (Riger 1992, p. 731). Bias in current scholarship is the application of inherently male positivist (traditional) scientific methods and the lack of attention to social context (Riger 1992; Gumport 1988). Harding challenges the neutrality of science and argues for inclusion of "the location of the knower":

> Feminist empiricism argues that the characteristics of the knower are irrelevant to the discovery process if the norms of science are followed. . . . [The] basis for a feminist standpoint epistemology is the argument that women's life experiences are not fully captured in existing conceptual schemes. Research often equates MALE with the general typical case, and considers FEMALE to be the particular — a subgroup demarcated by biology" (Harding in Riger 1992, p. 732).

Feminist postmodernism, which proposes that we are living in a new and different kind of world, and in particular poststructuralism, developed great influence for emerging scholarship. The central question in poststructuralism revolves around which values and social institutions are favored by each of the multiple versions of reality. Of crucial concern is identifying whose interests are served or maintained by the ways in which we give meaning to the world (Riger 1992). Feminist scholars argue that even the concepts used to understand organizational life (such as rationality and hierarchy) tend to be male-biased (Miller 1995).

Some academics, however, find they are torn between including feminist scholarship and the desire to avoid being associated with feminist scholarship. Association with feminist scholarship often means that faculty members will be characterized as producing "second-class" work (MacCorquodale and Linsink 1991). The devaluation of women's and feminist studies create a definition of being "other" for academics who seek to integrate and/or separately study feminist scholarship. Not surprisingly, women students find course material that includes women to be more attractive and more interesting. However, gender differences in faculty evaluations appear in classes where the curriculum includes feminist theory.

In a project comparing women's-studies classes and humanities classes in which feminized theory was introduced, the researchers found that female students are more likely than male students to perceive attitude toward the material as positive and three times as likely to rate the course as excellent if the professor's attitude was positive. But, male students were three times more likely than female students to see the instructors as hostile (MacCorquodale and Linsink 1991).

Student evaluations are included in decisions of tenure and promotion. In nonresearch institutions, the impact of these evaluations may be substantial, and in research institutions, student evaluations also may be utilized by the more traditional members as a gatekeeping tool used against those with new or different ideas about education.

Women's studies have taken many forms in the curriculum; however, the marginalized location in institutions renders women's studies as problematic for faculty. Association with feminist scholarship devalues one as "other" in the institution. Furthermore, feminist scholarship often is characterized as second-class work by traditional institutional members. Even though women students perceive feminist course material as positive and even excellent, issues of tenure, merit, recognition, and promotion rest upon one's academic vocation within the academy. This dilemma culminates in a difficult career decision for the faculty member who wants to appear to be attached to the academic culture rather than perceived as attached to a political movement.

The production of feminist scholarship as a primary academic vocation, then, becomes a risky career decision (Gumport 1991). Issues of merit and promotion rest with one's academic vocation and production of scholarship. Thus, whether the scholarly work is cutting edge, its radical edge renders it problematic nonetheless in that some view feminist theory as a political, not an academic, movement (Gumport 1991).

A feminist pedagogy provides more participatory and collaborative arrangements within the syllabus and also provides for exemplary models brought from a diverse offering in terms of gender, race, ethnicity, and social class.

Pedagogy

Scholarship, faculty, and curriculum cannot be fully discussed without discussing pedagogy and the dynamics that occur from classroom interaction. A natural outgrowth of feminist and women's studies is feminist pedagogy. Substantial research has been conducted and literature developed to address the perpetuation of gender bias within higher education classrooms and lecture halls when traditional pedagogy is in place.

Feminist pedagogy offers alternatives for classroom interaction and societal messages to the students. A feminist pedagogy provides more participatory and collaborative arrangements within the syllabus and also provides for exemplary models brought from a diverse offering in terms of gender, race, ethnicity, and social class. All students — particularly women and minority students — no doubt would benefit from more friendly, welcoming, and equality-based environments. The impact of the new feminist pedagogy upon male students has yet to be determined, however, for it has not been widely adopted as the science of teaching in academe.

Instructional practices and curriculum passed on through the ages, although often not intentionally or maliciously, provided encouragement for male students and, conversely, discouragement for female students. The concept of equality in the classroom cannot be met when faculty, who may be unaware of their subtly biased words and gestures, continue to include male-normed curriculum and bias practices in interaction with students. Bernice Sandler and Roberta Hall, formerly of the Association of American Colleges, coined the term "chilly climate" when they conducted a national study of classroom experiences for male and female college students in 1982. They found, for example, that faculty paid less attention to female students and tended to value their work less in comparison to male students. Sandler and Hall noted small behaviors, called "micro-inequities," occurring in the course of everyday interchanges between faculty and students (Henry and Stockdale 1995). A 1995 follow-up study by Sandler and Hall indicates these micro-inequities continue to be essentially unabated on college campuses.

A compilation of behaviors and gestures that are part of the hidden curriculum include:

- A tendency to have more eye contact with male students than female students as a sign of encouragement (Freeman 1989; Katz and Vieland 1988; Sandler and Hall 1982, 1986).
- Often asking female students more factual or concrete questions but more often requesting male students to respond to complex or analytical questions, thereby encouraging hierarchical thinking with male students (Henry and Stockdale 1995; Katz and Vieland 1988; Sandler and Hall 1982, 1986).
- Faculty often appearing to be distracted or engaged in other activities while a female student is speaking but exhibiting a tendency to have a more attentive stance while male students are speaking (Freeman 1989; Katz and Vieland 1988; Sandler and Hall 1982).
- Utilization of the generic man in texts and classroom examples and often using "he" when speaking of an exemplary individual but infrequently utilizing "she" (Shavlik and Touchton 1992; Gumport 1988).
- Allowing male students to interrupt female students as they either ask or respond to a question posed in the classroom (O'Banion 1989; Sandler and Hall 1982, 1986).
- Through commentary, encouraging male students to pursue their theories or philosophical debates, whereas female students have their theories dismissed as being philosophically naive or uniformed (Henry and Stockdale 1995; Fox 1989; Katz and Vieland 1988).
- In testing situations, women tend to be more successful and comfortable with collaborative efforts. This also is true for required classroom projects. Conversely, male students tend to be more comfortable with the traditional standard of independent work and work products as well as testing situations, and this continues to be the norm (O'Banion 1989).
- The tendency to give women less feedback than men, whether positive or negative, and ignoring women's comments at meetings and in other settings (Henry and Stockdale 1995).

- Focusing undue attention on a woman's personal life, appearance, and other personal qualities and relationships rather than on her accomplishments (Henry and Stockdale 1995; Sandler and Hall 1982, 1986).

Women who are the recipients of these micro-inequities have difficulty visualizing themselves as leaders in institutions in which they are identified as being less than equal. Just as leadership scholarship shows the generic man as the ideal, so too does the hidden curriculum in biased classroom environments. Women's perceptions of their roles in the classroom transfer into institutional and workplace understandings upon graduation. Organizational cultures and structures further reenforce the role perceptions of women both socially and organizationally (Ferguson 1984; Kanter 1977).

Personal, family, and career issues

Scholars who have investigated gender roles in contemporary society (for example, Thorne 1994; Blackmore 1993; Hensel 1991; Faludi 1991; Millett 1990; Tannen 1990; Fox 1989; Freeman 1989; Schaef 1985) have identified the existence of a long-term, historical social construction of gender. These scholars maintain that the position of women has been developed to sustain them in an oppressed status in society. In large part this position is due to the expectation of women as fulfilling the role of nurturer within the family structure. As nurturers, women are expected to prioritize their lives and goals accordingly. Both families and professional careers are "greedy" institutions but until changes occur, women who want both can expect to face conflicting and overwhelming demands (Kaufman 1989).

Throughout the centuries into the present, marriage continues to be a major concern for women. As recent as 1991, a *Time* magazine poll of young college women showed that a long marriage with healthy children was placed as a higher priority than a career (Bengiveno 1995). Although it is more socially acceptable for women to enter the workforce and develop careers, marital life still is viewed as the primary sphere of women in our society.

"A common gender stereotype is that women are less motivated than are men by a need for achievement, but research has not supported this notion. What research does suggest is that women . . . are faced with pressures to balance their achievement needs against their desire for relationships . . ." (Lips 1989, p. 208). These other directed aspirations continue into the woman's adult life and are reflected in choices made throughout her career. Women's achievements, whether home-related or professionally related, are socially devalued and only the "superachiever" is considered equal to a male. Yet, while we may speak about the importance of family, we don't really value the achievements of women in the family. This is further compounded by male coworkers, whether superiors, peers, or subordinates, who continue to hold traditional perceptions of women through deeply embedded socially constructed and socially normed roles.

Furthermore, most workplaces do not provide policies or procedures that take into account the different roles ascribed to gender in our society. Also compounding the workplace problems are those related to role ascription for women once in the workforce. Although women have made gains, the message remains that women and men are unequal. Women continue to learn that their proper role is one of subordination or support to men (Bengiveno 1995; also see England 1992 and Gutek 1989). Seidman's 1985 study of community college faculty, for example, found that women faculty expressed concern with sexist attitudes and the negative effect of these attitudes on their ability to obtain or succeed in leadership positions (in Townsend 1995).

Oftentimes a woman faces workplace decisions that are different than those of her male counterpart. As evidenced by data gleaned from *The College President: A 1993 Edition*, the difficult personal family and career decisions continue in a woman's life even when she holds a leadership position. In the 1990 presidential profile (Ross, Green, and Henderson 1993), 51 percent of female college presidents report being single compared with less than 10 percent of male presidents. This may be due to the need to delay or eliminate some difficult personal decisions that a marital and/or family situation might bring, although the data also could indicate lifestyle preferences not addressed in marriage-related questions. But, regardless of women's choices, "A successful professional career requires early achievement and uninterrupted competition for continued success — timing based on the male pattern" (Kaufman 1989, p. 338). Kaufman states that this is almost impossible based on the current status of women in families and in society.

A traditional organization is not tolerant of those who do not fit within the expected structure, norms, or ceremonies surrounding the institution. The childbearing and nurturing role of women in society has made it difficult for women to garner acceptance and gain entrance into roles that are historically held by males. Kandyoti chronicles how women "bargain with the patriarchy" at times to maintain traditional social roles while at other times attempting to reach comprise in these roles (1989).

A barrier to professional advancement not often addressed is the cost of child care for the single or divorced professional academic. To participate in committee work, community work, out-of-town presentations, or even to spend the time needed to conduct research and develop publishable materials, single women raising children must consider the high cost of child care — a cost not often considered by the institution or academics who have spouses or close family members to support their efforts. Few universities provide child-care assistance to their employees. The financial and emotional expense of locating quality child care exacts a price in the "career capital" expected to be expended by professionally serious members of academe (Bengevino 1995).

Finkel and Olswang conducted a study of assistant female professors employed at a large, public university classified as a Carnegie 1 Research University (1995). A questionnaire was sent to all 189 women in this category. Although a large majority were married (78.5 percent), 30 percent of the respondents in the study had decided never to have children. Of this number, 45.9 percent reported that their decision was greatly influenced by their career plans. More than half (55.4 percent) had children, but only 31 percent indicated that child care was shared equally with their spouses or partners. Further, more than half of the assistant professors with children (59.1 percent) reported that time required by children was a serious threat to tenure. (As stated earlier, single women, assumed to be childless, tended to have the highest rate of published books over their careers (Astin and Davis 1985). Of the 14 impediments to tenure identified in the questionnaire, *"these responses indicate that children play an important role in the lives of female assistant professors and is perceived as a serious threat to tenure for more female assistant professors than any of the fourteen impediments, including sexism or sexual harassment"* (Finkel and Olswang 1995, p. 149).

Historically, women have been expected to prioritize their goals based upon a primary role as nurturer in the family. Yet, a successful professional career requires timing based on the male pattern — that is, early achievements and uninterrupted competition. A common stereotype is that women are less motivated then men, but research has shown that in actuality women face traditional perceptions of sex roles; pressures to balance family and career needs; and financial, emotional, and time constraints related to child care. In turn, women express concern with resultant sexist attitudes which negatively affect their ability to obtain or succeed in faculty or leadership positions.

Sexual harassment

Personal and professional issues faced by women are compounded by the issues of sexual harassment and wage disparities. Although sexual harassment of working women historically has been as common as paychecks, women are becoming less willing to collude in its perpetuation. In 1980, sexual harassment was declared to be a violation of Title VII of the U.S. Civil Rights Act. At the same time, it was made clear that employers have a duty to prevent sexual harassment and to impose sanctions when it does occur (Schur 1984). However, it remains quite clear that sexual harassment can be anticipated in virtually any situation in which men and women interact. It is especially prevalent in work or education situations in which women are subject to male authority or supervision. For some women, the economic or academic consequences of confrontal behavior is severe: "It is not surprising then that most women are coerced into tolerance" (Schur 1984, p. 139).

Occupational power has much to do with sexual harassment of women. Whether the male perpetrator is a supervisor, a professor, or a colleague, harassing behavior "seeks to sustain both male workplace power and male power to treat women as sexual objects" (Schur 1984, p. 142; also Riger 1991; Katz and Vieland 1988; Nieva and Gutek 1980). This problem further is compromised by the general perception that what goes on between the sexes is personal rather than organizational (Gutek 1989; Schur 1984; Nieva and Gutek 1980). "Employers asserted it would be unfair to hold them responsible for the predictable consequences of these 'natural' conditions, and to do so would also have a chilling effect on amicable work relations between the sexes" (Schur 1984, p. 144).

Even though memoranda and policy statements from employers circulate among employees, these, too, create their own sets of problems. In particular, women and men typically view sexual harassment, personal confrontation, and sexual-harassment policies in different ways.

"Women perceive sexual harassment differently than men do, and their orientation to dispute resolution processes is likely to differ as well. The way that policies define harassment and the nature of dispute resolution procedures may better fit male than female perspectives" (Riger 1991, p. 497). Although it is women who face harassment at a much higher frequency than men (Riger 1991; Gutek 1989; Katz and Vieland 1988), dispute-resolution processes often favor mechanisms that are more comfortable for males (therefore the majority of offenders) than females. Most often the first step required in an established procedure is informal dispute resolution. This procedure does not always result in punishment for the offending behavior. The lack of negative consequences does little to deter the offender from harassing again.

In institutions of higher learning, the most common form of punishment reported is a verbal warning by a supervisor, which is given only 'sometimes.' Dismissal and litigation are almost never used. It seems likely, then, that sexual harassment may be viewed by potential harassers as low-risk behavior, and that victims see few incentives to bring official complaints (Riger 1991, p. 501).

Evidence of the continued persistence of sexual harassment is borne out in studies conducted across the country in work sites and educational institutions (for example, Riger 1991; Gutek 1989; Katz and Vieland 1988; Konrad and Gutek 1986; Nieva and Gutek 1980). Campus-climate surveys continue to indicate that harassing activities are part and parcel of campus life and where, on average, 40 percent of women have been recipients of sexist, insulting, or offending sexual behaviors from men (for example, University of Arizona 1994 campus climate survey; Riger 1991; Katz and Vieland 1988).

As women gain positions of authority and, in particular, leadership positions, and when policies and procedures reflect what victims deem to be appropriate resolutions, sexually harassing behaviors should abate. However, as long as current norms determine the boundaries of "problem behavior" and dispute-resolution policies and procedures, women will continue to be expected to subordinate their sense of fair and just resolutions to those who are in authority. As it stands, many would argue that the process is not neutral in that the law and resultant procedures see and treat women in the same way that men see and treat women.

Until sexual harassment in the workplace is perceived to be related to occupational power rather than attraction between the sexes, harassment will continue to be viewed as personal rather than organizational. An informal and "low-risk" dispute-resolution process indicates that sexual harassment is perceived as being an expected or even "natural" condition of work. Currently, the boundaries and procedures for this workplace problem appear to be defined in terms of what is most comfortable for men, even though women perceive sexual harassment differently than men. Women's leadership and authority is critical in redefining institutional standards, policies, and procedures to ensure harassing behavior is viewed as high-risk behavior and that tolerance for harassment is not coerced through threats of economic or academic consequences.

The wage gap
Resolution of the wage-gap issue also has become a test of the patience and sense of justice of women. Bellas analyzed data from a 1984 national survey sponsored by the Carnegie Foundation (1993). A sample population of 310 institutions gleaned a total of 5,057 useable responses. The results show that women faculty were earning approximately 25 percent less than faculty men. Of all the variables tested, except for hours spent in teaching, the differences always favored the men. And, perhaps not surprisingly, "Teaching appears to have a depressive effect on men's but no effect

on women's salaries" (Bellas 1993, p. 72), since work identified as being feminized repeatedly has been shown to be devalued (Volk 1995; Slaughter 1993; England 1992; Pfeffer and Davis-Blake 1987). In the Bellas study, when all other differences were controlled (such as level of education, rank, and professional achievement), even at an equivalent standing, women's salaries, on average, were 6.6 percent lower then faculty men's salaries. Through her findings, Bellas concludes that most variables that interacted with sex and wages were unrelated to performance of both men and women.

Bellas also found that disciplines with higher proportions of women faculty suffer a wage penalty. Bellas examined three propositions for the negative effect of women's salaries in academic disciplines: cultural devaluation of women and their work, labor market conditions, and characteristics of individual faculty (1994, in Volk 1995). She concluded that all three factors contribute to variations in faculty salaries, and that women faculty tend to be grouped in disciplines in which institutional salary differentials are the greatest.

According to the latest data from the U.S. Bureau of Labor Statistics, full-time female professors earn 86.6 percent of what males earn. But this is an improvement over 1979, when the proportion was only 79.4 percent (Wilson 1995). Recent pay-equity studies conducted in national higher education institutions show that the salary differences continue to be problematic. Examples of these salary differences: At the University of California at Davis, women earn about $3,000 less per year; at Kent State University, male professors earn as much as $3,288 more than women; Northern Arizona University provided annual pay raises ranging from $183 to $6,945 to women faculty to provide parity with male faculty; and Virginia Commonwealth University found an average wage gap of $1,900 (Wilson 1995).

A 1995 study of 11 colleges at the University of Arizona showed an annual salary difference between women and men of $5,200 in the college of education, $5,800 in science, $2,728 in the humanities, and up to $16,000 in the college of law. These gender-related salary differences were found to be statistically significant even when variables such as years of experience, rank, and educational background were accounted for (Wabnik 1995).

Bellas also found that disciplines with higher proportions of women faculty suffer a wage penalty.

Little information is available regarding institutions with established salary scales, for there appears to be an assumption that salary scales provide for equity-based pay. Yet, it is not without anecdotal evidence that salary scales that comprise steps and ranges allow for differential initial placement for entering faculty and administrators. One's initial placement within the pay scale, though, becomes the foundation for pay and pay increases during one's career in a particular institution.

From their first job, women usually are paid less than men, and across-the-board raises widen the gap. Johnsrud and Heck (in *Women in Higher Education*, April 1994) found that women who work their way up from instructor or adjunct-faculty positions often end up with lower salaries than men hired from outside an institution. Most often, the male faculty member was getting a higher salary elsewhere to begin with. Further, even when their experience and positions match, when a male faculty member is hired (at a higher rate) the woman's salary is not increased to create equity. Ultimately, and unfortunately, women then also have a lowered retirement income based on the cumulative effect of the salary disparity.

Volk conducted regression analyses of resource allocations over a five-year period in academic units of a research 1 university (1995). She found that gender and ethnicity (variables of diversity within a university department) often negatively affect the amount of resources allocated to the department. Volk speculates that this finding is "in accordance with the critical/political theory, which indicates that women and minorities are often considered subordinate to the male-dominant society" (Volk 1995, p. 123), and there is devaluation of work that primarily is performed by or associated with women.

As is the case with faculty salaries, women administrators in higher education also find there is a cost to being female. Pfeffer and Davis-Blake describe an institutionalized concept of "women's work" that includes the idea that work performed by women is less valuable and can be paid less than work by men, and that sets wages at a lower level for both men and women who occupy such positions (1987). Like other researchers who have conducted gender-equity studies (for example, England 1992), Pfeffer and Davis-Blake, utilizing a large data set of 18,861 higher education administrative positions, find that the proportion of women in an occupation, regardless of level, is negatively related to the prestige of the occupation. The researchers conclude that the data do not provide any current evidence of diminished stereotyping or reduced wage discrimination for women.

A comparable-worth salary plan, based upon the value of the job to the institution, is an equitable alternative to job classifications that are based on gender-related attributes of the position. However, the decision to support such a plan has a downside. If adopted, such a plan would increase the institution's salary obligation to its women employees (Tinsley, Secor, and Kaplan. 1984) since national studies consistently show that women in female-dominated job classifications and disciplines are paid less than men in male-dominated classifications (Bellas 1993; England 1992; Kelly 1991; Pfeffer and Davis-Blake 1987; Hartmann 1976). Because of the limited financial resources of most institutions, a comparable-worth salary plan has not been a high-priority item for most institutional administrators — male or female. Women, though, are becoming impatient with this notion; concurrently, some men forward the claim that seniority and/or scholarly productivity are valid reasons for the pay differences shown in salary-equity studies.

The wage penalty for being female has little to do with performance or institutional mission. Teaching, associated as being feminized, maintains women's salaries at lower levels then men's, and this includes disciplines dominated by female and minority students and faculty. Level of education, professional achievement, and years of experience of the incumbent have little to do with variations in faculty salaries. The wage gap also is found in administrative salaries.

Regardless of level, when a woman occupies an administrative position there is an apparent negative relationship between prestige and salary for the position. A comparable-worth salary plan, however, is not considered a workable solution since such a plan would strain the limited financial resources of most institutions. The negative influence on salaries due to women's participation in occupational roles leads to speculation about how women's participation will impact presidential salary levels as more women move into the highest-ranking leadership positions.

Evaluations of Occupational Prestige

A discussion of wage disparities and persistence factors in the leadership gender gap also needs to include the evaluations of occupational prestige. One argument forwarded regarding the relative exclusion of women in administrative-leadership roles relates to lowered occupational prestige as a result of women "contaminating" the role or position. Studies of various occupations have found that the proportion of women in an occupation is negatively related to prestige of the occupation. With a loss of prestige there also is a depression of income earned by both women and men. Pfeffer and Davis-Blake used large data sets of higher education administrative salaries for the years 1978 to 1983 (1987). Their findings indicate that: (1) A disparity exists between the wages of men and women administrators; (2) approximately 32 percent of the disparity relates to gender when other variables are controlled; and (3) the strongest argument for this disparity relates to institutionalization, which maintains there is a point at which work becomes defined as women's work.

Increases in the proportion of women around that point have much greater effect on wages than any other variable tested (Pfeffer and Davis-Blake 1987). Such a strong argument, validated with large data sets, begs several questions regarding the gender gap in higher education leadership. One of the obvious questions is whether women are virtually excluded from higher education leadership positions due to men's concerns about the potential feminizing of leadership roles, which then would lead to lowered prestige and economic value of the position.

Summary of Persistence Factors

The closing of the gender gap is more pressing than ever. Those at the helm need to be more representative of those in the ranks. The perpetuation of a male-dominated presidency no longer should be the norm if the majority populace it serves are women (Leatherman 1993; Schuster 1985).

Women received more than 44 percent of earned doctoral degrees in 1991 but make up only 32 percent of full-time faculty in higher education. Further, at doctoral-level universities, only 18 percent of full professors and 25 percent of associate professors are women (Finkel and Olswang 1995; Rigaux 1995; Hensel 1991). This disparity leads to an apparent skewing of proportionately more women than men who hold Ph.D.s in other types of institutions such as community colleges. This partially may explain why there are proportionately more women presidents in junior and community colleges than in public universities.

In 1995 almost 25 percent of academic officer positions were held by women (Rigaux 1995). However, more than half of the women holding academic dean positions were in nursing, home economics, arts and sciences, and continuing education (Wagner and DeFleur 1993) and each of these were shown to be lower-paid and at a higher risk during periods of retrenchment than typically male-dominated departments. In a 1990 study of community colleges, less than 10 percent of the 1,169 academic deans listed with the American Association of Community and Junior Colleges, or AACJC, were found to have women's first names (Vaughan 1990). Ironically, perhaps, in the 1990 presidential profile the majority of all presidents previously had held a post as chief academic officer in a higher education institution.

A 1983 study of higher education administrative positions found that the largest number of women were employed as head librarian, registrar, and director of financial aid (Tinsley et al. 1984). And, "It is commonly believed that once launched in a given [career] track, individuals do not move easily to another" (Tinsley et al. 1984).

Women "in the pipeline" for formal leadership positions is somewhat an institutional myth when the data are more closely scrutinized. Even when women are more highly educated, they still receive lower pay than men and are less likely to be promoted into leadership positions (Anderson 1988). It is little wonder, then, that women's returns on investment in education do not equal those of men beginning with salary levels and promotional opportunities and culminating in reduced retirement income (Leslie and Brinkman 1988; Anderson 1988).

Compounding the problematic persistence factors in the leadership gap is the informal network system from which women, for the most part, have been excluded. It often is these networks from which insider information is gained and hiring and promotional decisions are determined. The higher a woman rises in an organization, the more difficulty she faces as she tries to fit in because "most men highest up work with few women regularly and socialize with female staff members even less" (Milwid 1990, p. 77). When excluded from an informal network system the implications are serious: Women become isolated while decisionmakers are kept unaware of their competence.

Social exclusion hurts women's careers most because it limits their exposure to managers at the top. Without a relaxed atmosphere in which to meet leaders, female professionals have no access to policymakers other than through their work (Milwid 1990, p. 82).

When cut off informally, the opportunities for attaining a leadership position in an institution are severely curtailed. Further, this type of exclusion removes women from decisionmaking spheres. As a result, women await announced policy decisions rather than being active players in the decisionmaking process. It is important to note that it is not the actual structure that defines a sense of climate but rather the perceptions and understandings these structures create (Kanter 1977). Organizational members develop perceptions of the practices, policies, and customs of the organization, and these perceptions are critical to the discovery and management of campus climate. It also is climate that determines how the previously listed persistence factors and barriers in the gender gap are understood and managed by campus personnel. To manage the culture, an institution leadership must define the attitudes, values, and expectations they want organizational members to share (Lussier 1993). Yet traditionally, organizational culture is designed to influence people's attitudes, not the organization's structure. Culture teaches new members within the organization the correct way to perceive, think, and feel in relation to the organization and organizational policies and procedures (Miller 1995; Trice and Beyer 1993).

Although an institution's culture may be designed to be exclusionary in its practices (such as tenure criteria, pedagogy, wage level, sexual-harassment policies, or production and acceptance of scholarship), "true believers" in the culture hold at bay those who question or challenge existing norms. "Ideology influences the way we perceive the world and involves assumptions that are rarely questioned or scrutinized" (Miller 1995, p. 134). Thus, many members remain

Changes initiated in unsupportive cultural environments are doomed to fade or fail over time.

passive observers of an institution's ideology that controls organizational discourse and gender relationships. Unfortunately, hegemony, a process in which a dominant group defines and protects the group's norms through the subordination of others, is the result of unquestioned ideology.

In the 1960s, Betty Friedan encouraged women to refuse to be passive and work toward living a self-chosen life. As other activists have shown us throughout history, the path to change is by transforming passive observers to active players. To change campus climates, professional barriers, and gender-gap persistence factors, women and men interested in equality must continue to challenge current policies, procedures, and institutional norms.

Individual initiative is a necessary ingredient for change (Allen and Allen 1987). Organizing those who are concerned with these issues is a first step in creating active players from passive observers. Changes initiated in unsupportive cultural environments are doomed to fade or fail over time. Further, both the willingness to attempt to change and long-term success are positively related to cultural support. Therefore, to achieve sustained results, a long-term solution also must be a cultural solution (Allen and Allen 1987).

GENDER THEORY AS A FORM OF EMERGING LEADERSHIP THEORY

At least two questions are important to ask with respect to the roles of women and men as leaders. First, do men and women lead in the same way? And second, when women lead in institutions of higher education, are their institutional environments different from those that are led by men? Some completed studies provide a basis for comparing women and men as leaders.

Power and Leadership

Leadership is equated to power (Melia and Lyttle 1986; Cuming 1985) and unless women become more effective power users in higher education, say Leonard and Sigall, the academy will remain under a male-dominant system (1989). Leaders influence people to do things through the use of power and authority. "Power is the ability to influence decisions and control resources. . . . Authority is the formal right to get people to do things or the formal right to control resources" (DuBrin 1994, p. 264).

Various studies on gender differences in power orientation have shown some variations in perspectives of power between women and men. A major factor lies in the definition of power. "Women tend to view power as a means to promote change, whereas men tend to view power as a means to having influence over other people - 'power to' versus 'power over'" (Kelly 1991, p. 101).

Gilligan's female interviewees equated power with giving and care and portrayed acts of nurturing as acts of strength (1982). Schaef states, "In the White Male System, power is conceived in a zero-sum fashion. In the Female System, power is seen as limitless" (1985, p. 124). Schaef explains that men's concept of power is based on a scarcity model, whereas women view power as something that increases when given away.

Patton reports that women managers in higher education are less interested in power and control; rather, they perceive their leadership roles to be facilitative, relational, and contributory to the institution (1990). Northcutt also finds that women define career success without a power orientation and that women focus more on contributing to society and to others (1991).

Milwid discovered in interviews with professional women that power was not viewed as a right of position but rather was seen as a commodity which, when shared, grew rather than depleted (1990). One of Milwid's women presidents succinctly states, "Power is something people give you in relation to how you make them feel about themselves. . . . Real power comes when you're strong enough to make your employees feel good about themselves and their work" (p. 130).

Traditional, postmodern, and feminist scholars agree that there are two sources of power: positional and personal. Positional power is derived from one's title or status in the organization and can be delegated through the chain of command. "Personal power is largely due to one's personality. Leaders with personal power get it from followers because they meet their needs" (Lussier 1993, p. 291). The type of power the leader utilizes is indicative of preferred leadership style.

Women's Leadership Style

Sally Helgesen chronicled the leadership styles of four women chief executive officers (1990). Through these case studies, she examined how women make decisions, gather and disperse information, delegate tasks, structure their companies, and motivate their employees. Helgesen utilized Mintzberg's methodology, following executives through their days and using a diary approach to record their minute-by-minute activities.

Helgesen also used Mintzberg's results as a standard against which she compared her women leaders. Minzberg studied five male executives and emphasized the pattern of activities these men followed. Mintzberg's men were found to focus on completing tasks, achieving goals, and winning. Helgesen's women executives did not view encounters as interruptions. The women scheduled time to share information, whereas Mintzberg found the men tended to hoard information. Helgesen claims her diary studies show the women leaders to be caring, helpful, and involved, with an emphasis on relationships, sharing, and process. Ultimately, she views Mintzberg's men as "less reflective and deliberate, narrower" (Helgesen 1990, p. 29). The case-study research conducted by Helgesen and utilizing Mintzberg's study for female and male comparison is somewhat akin to the Gilligan/Kohlberg ethical-dilemma research comparisons of moral development in males and females.

A widely recognized theory in gender differences is proposed by Carol Gilligan (1989, 1982). Gilligan argues that the unitary model based on male subjects and which traditionally has been accepted fails to capture the different reality of women's lives. By positing two different reasoning modes, a more complex but more understandable rendition of human experience can be contemplated. Her theory of women's cognitive development "emphasizes the relationships between people and a concern for preventing psychological or physical harm" (Wilcox and Ebbs 1992, p. 46). Gilligan refers to this as the "care voice" (response mode) for women as opposed to the "justice voice" (rights mode) for men (1982).

Kohlberg's six-stage theory, based on research conducted with young men, was challenged by Gilligan as being inappropriate for women's development. The justice voice, ascribed to males, stresses separation and detachment and considers the individual rather than the relationship as primary (Kuk 1990). Although the two voices (modes) are gender-related, they are not gender-specific. All people behave in both modes (voices) but when presented with dilemmas, people will show a preference to respond out of one voice (Desjardins 1989; Gilligan, Ward, and Taylor 1989; Gilligan 1982). Care-voice individuals "prefer collaborative discussion and learning by listening" (Wilcox and Ebbs 1992, p. 47), tend to be more relationship-based negotiators who have concern for others, and balance the needs and wants of all parties (Gilligan 1982). While men are more concerned about rules, women are more concerned about relations. And, as found by Chodorow, men's social orientation is positional, while women's is personal. This separate development pathway results in personal responsibility as being of highest value for females and legalistic equality being highest for males.

The Myers and Briggs typographical profile somewhat confirms Gilligan's observed differences.

Men and women score equally on all major dimensions of the instrument with the exception of decision making. In this area, men fall predominantly within the 'thinking' category for decision making, being more comfortable with following rules, laws, formulas and the like, and subordinating relationships to principles. Women, on the other hand, are more likely to fall into the 'feeling' category, where decisions are based on relationships and personal outcomes (Edge and Groves 1994, p. 6).

Also confirming Gilligan's observations, in a meta-analysis of "Gender and the Emergence of Leaders," Eagly and Karau found that in originally leaderless groups, men emerged as leaders to a greater extent than did women; in contrast, women emerged as social leaders slightly more than did men (1991). Eagly and Johnson conducted a meta-analysis of gender and leadership style and found a range of writings from those who argue for the presence of sex differences to those who encourage androgynous managers (1990). Although not statistically prominent, there was some confidence that women's leadership styles emphasize both interpersonal relations and task accomplishment at a slightly greater extent than men's styles (Eagly and Johnson 1990). (From later studies, this finding may be attributed to perceptions of male coworkers and employees, who perceive women to be more task-oriented regardless of the woman's task orientation).

However, the strongest evidence of sex difference in leadership style related to women adopting a more democratic or participative style, whereas men tended to adopt a more autocratic or directive style. Milwid found this to be the case with the professional women she interviewed; increased employee involvement was the most commonly cited avenue for decisionmaking (1990). Others, though, argue that most women leaders either adopt behaviors or appear to behave in a similar fashion to their male colleagues due to organizational structures and normative reinforcements (Acker 1991; Northcutt 1991; Nieva and Gutek 1981; Kanter 1977). Milwid (1990) and Sheppard (1992) found that the women in their studies experienced organizational life with deep ambivalence due to these conflicting values and modes.

In 1996 a survey was conducted by Chliwniak with higher education leaders. Included in the survey were chancellors, presidents, provosts, vice chancellors, vice presidents, and deans. Of the 386 respondents, 149 were women and 247 were men.

Utilizing the "Traditional and Emerging Leadership Values and Modes" chart she developed as a guide (Table 2), Chliwniak attempted to discern if there were differences or gradations in perceptions of leader values and leadership modes based on gender, age, institutional type, years of experience, educational background, and/or position. Through correlational and factorial analyses, Chliwniak

TABLE 2
Traditional and Emerging
Leadership Value and Modes Continuum

Values, individually held by leaders, are exhibited through the leadership mode adopted by the individual. In turn, the leader's values and leadership mode become absorbed into the institution's culture and norms.

This table is based on dominant **values** held by traditional leaders at one end and emerging leaders at the other end. The second table describes dominant leadership **modes** of traditional leaders at one end and emerging leaders at the other end of the continuum.

Mixed-mode or integrated-mode leaders show only slight or no preference for one mode over the other.

TRADITIONAL	CONTINUUM TO	EMERGING
VALUES		
Individuality		Connection
Ambition		Cooperation
Desire to Win		Desire for Peaceful Environment
"Tough but Fair"		"Protect From Harm"
Life Is a Contest		Life Is in a Community
People Are Rivals		People Are Partners
Power = Calling the Shots		Power = Facilitating Change
Justice/Principles		Non-Violence/Care
Rules		Compassion
Systems		Climates
Autonomy		Intimacy
Rights of Others		Needs of Others
Discipline		Creativity
Command and Control		Empowerment
Obligation/Commitment		Interconnectedness
"Be Loyal"		"Be Supportive"
Principle Based		Situation Based
Individual Initiative		Participation
Authority		Consensus
Efficiency		Acceptance
Self-Confidence		Team Player
Completion of Tasks		Relationships With People
Legalistic Equality		Personal Responsibility

TRADITIONAL	CONTINUUM TO	EMERGING

MODES

Mechanistic	Wholistic
Hierarchy	Network
Leadership From the Top	Leadership From the Center
Promotes Fairness	Promotes Welfare
Information Is Controlled	Information Is Available
Focus on Results	Focus on Communication
Establishes Objectives	Listens to Concerns
Focus on Plans	Focus on Values
Focus on External Image	Focus on Internal Members
Power Is Scarce	Power Is Limitless
Positional Orientation	Personal Orientation
Negotiates Status	Creates Rapport
Military Archetype	Teaching Archetype
Issues Orders	Is a Role Model
Outcomes Oriented	Process Oriented
Analytical	Synthesizing
Deductive Thinking	Inductive Thinking
Individual Orientation	Relationship Orientation
Authoritarian	Inclusive
Orchestrates Strategy	Fluid Leadership
Plays "Hardball"	Facilitates
Bluntness	Diplomacy
Self-Promotion	Group Harmony
Verbal Bantering	Personal Information
Issues Challenges	Asks Questions
Aggressiveness	Cooperation

This table was developed by Luba Chliwniak (1995) as a compilation of behaviors and characteristics described by various traditional, posthierarchical, and feminist scholars who discuss leadership theory, cultural theory, and/or organizational theory. Sources include but are not limited to: Helgesen 1995, 1990; Kearney and White 1994; Tannen 1994, 1990; Blackmore and Kenway 1993; Aburdene and Naisbitt 1992; Eagly, Makhijani, and Klonsky 1992; Bergquist 1992; Garfield 1992; Sheppard 1992; Covey 1991; Eagly and Karau 1991; Bennis 1991; Reskin 1991; Fryer and Lovas 1991; Eagly and Johnson 1990; Milwid 1990; Gutek 1989; Birnbaum 1989; Hanna 1988; Burton 1987; Schaef 1985; Ferguson 1984; MacCoby 1981; Kanter 1977.

found that gender and position were highly correlated to leadership perceptions, whereas institutional type indicated fewer correlations to leadership perceptions. Age, years of experience, and educational background provided some influencing patterns. Chliwniak concludes that although leadership perceptions are not necessarily dependent upon gender and that position is shown to be statistically significant in the perceptions of the survey subjects, women do appear to exhibit emerging (response mode) perceptions of leadership to a greater degree than do men when write-in responses are analyzed utilizing gender theory rather than leadership theory as a basis for textual analysis. Based on the statistical outcomes, however, the gender gap in leadership has more to do with inequity than with variation in how leadership is perceived.

Sheryl Bond and a team of researchers from the University of Manitoba (Berkowitz 1996) studied leadership experiences and perceptions of Canadian university leaders. They conclude that positional power appears to have the greatest influence upon the views of leaders. Results based on quantitative data indicate women and men leaders appear to be more alike than different when position is the primary variable studied. However, Bond has not yet analyzed the qualitative portion of the surveys and is withholding final analysis of the national study until these survey responses also are taken into account. Cynthia Epstein concludes that her research indicates that gender differences are not empirically real (1988). Epstein posits that because gender differences are socially constructed, we believe there to be differences and perpetuate this belief through differences in our language and imagery.

Communication Patterns
Women and men develop distinctly different communication styles, often the result of social conditioning. Because of women's existence in a male-dominant culture, women learn linguistic adaptation for socially normed roles. Of particular interest in the study of higher education is women's tendency to switch from women's to neutral language once they spend some time in college (Samovar and Porter 1995).

Women's communication pattern generally is used to elicit cooperation or create rapport; men use conversation to negotiate status and often engage in verbal competition in which points of discussion are made in a definitive and forceful fashion (Samovar and Porter 1995). Deborah Tannen studies sociolinguistic patterns of men and women in relationships and at work (1990, 1994). She posits that when at work, "conversational rituals common among women are often ways of maintaining an appearance of equality . . . and expending effort to downplay the speaker's authority. . ." (Tannen 1994, p. 23). This strategy, though, often leaves women appearing as if they lack confidence and competence.

Men's conversational rituals involve using opposition in an effort to avoid the one-down position in the interaction. Women tend to ask more questions, whereas men are less likely to ask questions in a public situation when a lack of knowledge may appear to be a one-down position for the man.

Tannen (1994) and Thorne (1994) found that gender-related communication patterns constrain how girls and women express leadership. "Many girls discover they get better results if they phrase their ideas as suggestions rather than orders, and if they give reasons for their suggestions in terms of the good of the group" (Tannen 1994, p. 39). Groups of boys tend to be more obviously hierarchical with challenges and jockeying for the high-status position in the group (Thorne 1994). The result of these two behavioral patterns is that girls and women who appear authoritative are considered "bossy," whereas boys and men who take command are viewed as "go-getters." Bossy girls, though, are not accepted by either boys' or girls' groups and are considered somewhat deviant for accepted male/female norms and patterns. However, "go-getters" are accepted by both boys' and girls' groups.

When communication is constrained, it is difficult to exhibit an aura of competence or confidence while attempting to maintain an appearance of equality. It can be interpreted that the woman lacks authority or power traditionally associated with leadership positions. From a young age, girls and women are socialized to engage in communication patterns that create rapport, establish relationships, and elicit cooperation. Unwittingly, women continue to expect these communication patterns from other women at the work site and downgrade the women who do not follow the expected norm. The result is that women in leadership positions, regardless of competence levels, are not supported by either women or men when they appear to carry out their leadership role in an assertive or definitive manner (Johnson 1993; Eagly, Makhijani, and Klonsky 1992; Schaef 1985). This poses quite a dilemma for women who aspire to leadership positions, for historical cultural norming dictates an image of successful leadership that includes assertiveness, decisiveness, and authority. Women must choose whether to challenge social norms or become socialized to fit traditional, often masculinized, organizational expectations of leaders.

Career Satisfaction

Sex-role orientation and career satisfaction was measured by Adams with 53 women chief student-services officers and chief instructional officers working in California community colleges (1995). Her data indicate an association between sex-role orientation and intrinsic job satisfaction. Forty-nine percent of respondents identified an androgynous orientation (equally masculine and feminine traits); 38 percent fell into the masculine orientation category. These were the women who showed most intrinsic job satisfaction. Androgyny was most heavily represented in the 46 to 50 age group, and masculine orientation was represented in age groups above 45. Gloria Steinem reports on psychological tests that show androgynous individuals, males with more feminine qualities, and females with more masculine qualities tend to be more flexible and have healthier self-esteem (1994). However, homogeneity of gender-related characteristics or androgyny are concepts not encouraged in mass culture or in our social institutions. A more polarized approach to gender and gender roles appears to be the preferred and acceptable norm for socialization.

Adams recommends that women who aspire to administrative positions should cultivate masculine skills that may be lacking so that intrinsic job satisfaction can be increased (1995). However, Adams did not study variables for extrinsic satisfaction even though a high proportion of subjects in the androgynous category also fell into the highest salary category. Previous studies indicate that reliance on extrinsic rewards as traditional signals of success have been challenged by women. Murray's study, for example, found that job satisfaction for women in higher education was dependent upon motivators such as job level, tenure, and department (1986). Although position and advancement were perceived as important to job satisfaction, women valued intrinsic rewards more. Furthermore, women more often openly endorse efforts that develop family, community, and the cooperative enactment of organization and society (Refkind and Harper 1995).

The Glass Ceiling

Subtle, indirect obstacles as a result of labeling and stereotyping place stumbling blocks in the career paths of many women. Organizational glass ceilings are not due to the inability of women to function effectively in their responsibilities. Rather, the glass ceiling most often is the result of a woman being unlike her predecessor, usually a white male (Milwid 1990; Kanter 1977).

Studies have documented men's resistance to women entering "their" jobs (Eagly, Makhijani, and Klonsky 1992; Schroedel 1985; Hartmann 1976). Reskin's thesis posits that men respond to this intrusion in the workforce by emphasizing how men and women differ (1991). Further, the emphasis on the "natural" gender roles for women attempts to preserve "appropriate" and different spheres that are allocated to these roles, and the dominant group (men) has a stake in maintaining the differentiation of spheres (Reskin and Roos 1990).

According to Kandiyoti, the male-dominant system provides baselines from which women negotiate and strategize through "patriarchal bargains," sometimes negotiating to keep patriarchal norms intact — therefore gender roles and social norms intact (see also Amey and Twombly 1992) and sometimes compromising on the norms (1991).

Through intact patriarchal structures, men in organizations have come to view their perspectives and norms as being representative of gender-neutral human organizational structures (Acker 1991; Milwid 1990; Millett 1990; Gutek 1989) and assume the structure is asexual. Gutek coined the term "sex-role spillover" to describe how women's traditional roles were incorporated into patriarchal organizational structures (1989). Sheppard found that these male filters rendered women's experiences as invisible (1992; see also Burton 1987). And, "given the long history of the subordination of women's to men's interests, men's interests must be sacrificed" (Baier 1993, p. 24) if women's interests are to become primary or equal.

Steinem states that a remedial vision of the world — that is, one that is not seen through the eyes of only males —

> *Organizational glass ceilings are not due to the inability of women to function effectively in their responsibilities. Rather, the glass ceiling most often is the result of a woman being unlike her predecessor, usually a white male.*

would add depth and new perspectives for shared images of societal and organizational structures (1994). However, since 84 percent of higher education presidents, 83 percent of business officers, and 75 percent of academic deans are male, remedial vision would require a totally different makeup in academe's leadership ranks to communicate visible and continuing commitments to workforce diversity.

Studies that indicate androgynous or masculine orientations for women (for example, Adams 1995) and gender similarities in leadership due to position (for example, Bond 1996; Chliwniak 1996; Epstein 1988) imply that the gender gap may be more related to inequity than to difference. That is, holding a leadership position may influence, nullify, and/or socialize women's perception of leadership so women and men are more alike than different due to positional power. Furthermore, those in leadership positions are reflective of a funneled group of individuals who remained competitive through acculturation and socialization into institutional norms. The gender gap, therefore, would be related more to images of leadership and stereotypical gender roles than the ability or behavior of the incumbent.

Perhaps the greatest gender differences lie in how men and women are stereotyped or labeled within organizations and the evaluation criteria utilized to determine their effectiveness as a leader or the leadership style they have adopted. Women must deal with these stereotypes to a greater extent than men. In particular, conceptions associated with leadership cause great difficulty. Traditional, masculine behaviors expected of leaders — aggressiveness and authority, for example — are not associated as being feminized qualities. Thus, a woman may not "look like" or "act like" a dean, vice president, or president to those charged with making leadership selections, and the assumption that males have a "right" to or natural affinity for leadership remains a guidepost for selection committees (Mitchell 1993).

Naisbitt and Aburdene state that many of the new models for reinventing organizations stem from the impact of women in the workforce (1985). Further, they refer to Alice Sargent's message in *The Androgynous Manager* (1981). Namely,

> *Men and women should learn from one another without abandoning successful traits they already possess.*

Men can learn to be more collaborative and intuitive yet remain results-oriented. Women need not give up being nurturing in order to learn to be comfortable with power and conflict (1985, p. 207).

AN ANALYSIS OF LEADERSHIP: INDIVIDUAL, ORGANIZATIONAL, AND SOCIETAL CONCEPTUALIZATIONS

Introduction to Leadership Conceptualizations

The phenomenon of effective leadership is under constant scrutiny by scholars as well as practitioners. The characteristics and context of effective leadership appears to change over time as societal values shape what is acceptable, laudable, and effective. Further, conceptualizations of how leadership impacts organizational values and structures also vary according to authors' assumptions. This section provides an analysis of individual characteristics, organizational structures, and societal conceptions that have shaped what we determine to be effective leadership. With a focus primarily on gender-related aspects of leadership, these issues are placed in a context of traditional as well as current organizational structuring and norming.

What Is Leadership?

Warren Bennis points out, "Many an institution is very well managed and very poorly led" (1991, p. 17). He further states that the distinction between leaders and managers is, "Leaders are people who do the right thing; managers are people who do things right" (p. 18). "A reciprocal relationship exists between leadership and management, but leaders are not always good managers and managers are not always good leaders (Bruhn 1993, p. 40).

Whereas managers manage boundaries, leaders transcend boundaries and are innovative in their approaches. Although both functions are important to an institution, it is a common notion that leaders are the individuals who establish the culture and provide vision and meaning for an institution (Bryman 1992; Bennis 1991; Roueche, Baker, and Rose 1989; Bolman and Deal 1984; Gleazer 1980; Baldridge et al. 1977) and embody the ideals toward which an organization strives (Garfield 1992; Wilcox and Ebbs 1992; Wall, Solum, and Sobol 1992; Covey 1991).

Two leadership styles have become dominant in the literature. They can be envisioned as a place on a leadership continuum with autocratic leaders at one end and participative leaders at the other. Autocratic leaders maintain most of the power, authority, and control within the organization, whereas participative leaders engage organizational members through consultative or democratic processes (see Table 2).

Vroom and Yetton's Normative Leadership Theory identifies five situational leadership styles: Two are autocratic, two are consultative, and one is group-oriented. A decision tree, with eight questions, informs the leader about which style would be most appropriate in a specific situation. Therefore, the leader is expected to adapt a style based on the people and situation (Lussier 1993). This is referred to as situational leadership, where the situation dictates the style rather than someone maintaining one style of leadership regardless of the situation with which she or he is dealing.

Jane Gallimore-McKee provides an analysis of institutional leadership styles based on the perceptions of faculty regarding their chief executive officer: high task/high relationship, high task/low relationship, low task/high relationship, and low task/low relationship (1991). Of the four styles surveyed, the style perceived by faculty as being most prevalent among presidents is the high task/high relationship, which focuses on relationship building and attention to task accomplishment. When combined with the job satisfaction scale, the high relationship/low task style for a president was found to be the one that faculty most preferred for their own job satisfaction. This style is developed through "concentration on building a relationship of support and concern for individuals, removal of obstacles, and recognition of subordinate contributions" (p. 39). Gallimore-McKee states that this style requires the empowerment of followers developed through participatory leadership and shared governance; a leadership mode found in an emerging or feminized leadership style.

Transformational leadership is another important dimension in leadership theory. Transformational leadership is especially critical to the reformation and/or revitalization of an organization. "The transformational leader develops visions for the organization and mobilizes the employees toward attaining these visions" (DuBrin 1994, p. 280). Further, the transformational leader utilizes charisma and referent power to overhaul an organization's culture (1994). Referent power relies on personality and relationship with employees to gain acceptance for these changes (Lussier 1993).

Societal Conceptualizations
Michael MacCoby in *The Leader* provides a perspective of society's expectations and acceptance of past, current, and future leaders (1981). It is his belief that the older models of leadership, the basis of training in many universities across the country, will cease to work in our postindustrial society.

In an age of individual rights, paternal protectors ap-
pear patronizing. In an age of limits, seductive
promises fall flat. In an age of self-expression, even
rational authority may seem oppressive. Searching for
new direction, but critical of anyone who controls us,
we look for new leaders, as much in fear that we will
find them as that we will not (p. 23).

Burt Nanus describes several qualities of effective leadership
but states these are sorely lacking in America today (1989).
He states, "Americans perceive a leadership void that puts at
risk our traditions, our livelihoods, our lifestyles, our future,
and almost everything else we value. A new age of leadership is essential, worthwhile, and achievable" (p. 195).

Nanus seeks a renaissance of American leadership and
states that the educational system faces the greatest challenge in this quest. As a result of portrayals on television
and movie screens, students have come to view leaders as
charismatic manipulators pursuing selfish power goals rather
than as effective visionaries. Nanus suggests that leadership
development should begin in the classroom with supple-
mental off-campus experiences. It is his perception that few
teachers or college faculty know much about leadership and
the multidisciplinary approach needed for this topic. He
encourages administrators to give high priority to this subject and support efforts to improve faculty's ability to recognize, motivate, and enhance leadership skills. The media,
Nanus says, also must play a role in portraying positive leaders and leadership styles and take more responsibility in
whom they choose to celebrate and applaud.

The economics of the labor market also is indicative of
society's conceptions of who should be chosen and cele-
brated as leaders. It can be contended that a segmented
market directly impacts women's opportunities for administrative and leadership positions. Kelly utilizes segmented
labor-market theory to analyze the overall gendered picture
of the U.S. economy and the perpetuation of sex-segregation
in the U.S. labor force (1991).

Kelly finds that many factors contribute to women's success or failure in attaining equality with men in administrative and leadership positions. One of the greatest inhibitors
is the requirement that women follow male models of career
advancement — an impossibility in a segregated labor mar-

ket. Kelly describes how the political and social meaning of gender and work are highly interrelated and how this relationship substantially affects the structure of the labor market. She cites data that indicate that in only five of 12 labor sectors were there more than 5 percent of women in top positions. These include: foundations, 14.7 percent; universities, 10.6 percent; civic and cultural organizations, 9.0 percent; government, 7.7 percent; and mass media, 6.8 percent (1991). Quite noticeably, relatively few women have penetrated the upper echelons of society's labor market and caused impact upon the economy.

Blackmore and Kenway provide readers with a feminist introduction for contemplating educational administration in a societal context (1993). In their view, as education began to be taken over by the state and became more closely connected to the economy, men became dominant in the education system and acted as "gatekeepers" in setting standards, producing social knowledge, and decreeing what is significant, relevant, and important for others within the system. Included in the role of gatekeeper is the development of cultural perspectives for the institution, and embedded within the organization are dominant masculinist images of leadership that result in the exclusion of women. In turn, woman's role becomes that of a "caretaker," a subordinate position in a bureaucratic structure (Ferguson 1984).

Other feminist scholars (Aufderheid 1992; Gutek 1989; Pearson, Shavlik, and Touchton 1989; Anderson 1988; Burton 1987; Schaef 1985; and Gornick 1977) also note the phenomenon that purports leaders to be heterosexual, white, competitive, rational, and male. Historically and socially constructed manifestations of maleness and femaleness have played a significant, albeit detrimental, role in the interplay of skills and images within the workplace in gendered ways. The result has been an unchallenged and hegemonic image embodied in these principles and structures of administration (Blackmore and Kenway 1993).

Women are left to discover strategies that could or would provide for equal leadership opportunities and neutral procedures to evaluate merit and ability. This fertile ground is where the seeds are sown to envision what Ferguson describes as "a nonbureaucratic collective life" (1984, p. 26), an egalitarian social organization that replaces bureaucratic and hierarchical forms of organizational structures with participatory membership.

The Relevance of Gender in Leadership Conceptualizations

Culture is defined as "the set of definitions of reality held in common by people who share a distinctive way of life." Culture is, in essence, a pattern of expectations about what are appropriate behaviors and beliefs for the members of society (Anderson 1988, p. 74). Two internal cultural tasks, according to Schein, are to develop criteria for the allocation of status, power, and authority and to develop group boundaries and criteria for inclusion (1990). Institutional culture of academe has supported a social matrix that delineates roles, expectations, and aspirations for its members by structuring barriers for some and opening doors for others. Gender appears to have played a significant role in the development of this matrix.

Gender is an achieved status constructed through psychological, cultural, and social means (West and Zimmerman 1991; Millet 1990; Lips 1989; Eichenbaum and Orbach 1982). The power of gender classifications sustains, reproduces, and renders legitimate the institutional arrangements based on sex category (Faludi 1991; West and Zimmerman 1991; Acker 1991; Thorne 1994, 1989; Ferguson 1984). Role theory attends to the social construction of gender categories creating learned and enacted gender roles (West and Zimmerman 1991; Acker 1991; Thorne 1994, 1989). "Whenever people face issues of allocation — who is to do what, get what, plan or execute action, direct or be directed, incumbency in significant social categories such as 'female' and 'male' seems to become pointedly relevant" (West and Zimmerman 1991, p. 29). Organizational arrangements carry the supposed natural differences into the workplace and in doing so, men are expected to hold dominant positions while women provide deference and support (Kelly 1991; West and Zimmerman 1991; Gutek 1989).

Kanter, in *Men and Women of the Corporation*, argues that it is not the characteristics of men and women that create gender differences in organizational behavior, but it is due to the complex structure of the organization (1977). Gender is an issue when organizational roles "carry characteristics and

Kanter, in Men and Women of the Corporation, argues that it is not the characteristics of men and women that create gender differences in organizational behavior, but it is due to the complex structure of the organization.

images of the kinds of people that should occupy them" (Kanter 1977, p. 250); a phenomenon later dubbed "interior colonization" by Millett (1990). This translates to a crowding of women in low-paying, dead-end jobs at the bottom of the hierarchical structure (England 1992; Kelly 1991; Kanter 1977) and the positive evaluation of male workers, regardless of their position in the organization (Acker 1991).

Acker's research (1991) concludes that in the abstract, a gender-neutral job has no sex or emotion or procreation ability, while in reality the abstract worker is male and the lower ranking of women in organizations is justified by identification of women with domestic life, child bearing, and emotionality.

Carolyn Desjardins discusses the meaning of Gilligan's "different voice" through cognitive development and its implications in higher education organizations (1989). She points out that early in the women's movement, the assimilation of women into organizational cultures and structures was the goal. This was especially sought as the answer to the legal and social pressures compelling organizations to provide equal opportunity in response to equity issues. However, success became equated with male behaviors. Desjardins encourages women who strive to be successful in organizations to restate their thinking and think of themselves as women rather than as "honorary males" or sexless humans. Women and men in organizations cannot continue to conflate sameness with equality (Minnich 1989). It is through work such as Gilligan's that a different locus of thought is pursued.

Gilligan found in her research that men tended to envision the world in terms of ladders, while women were more likely to emphasize nets or webs of human connectedness. Men aspire to making it to the top of the ladder; women fear the isolation at the top. Women aim to encourage communication and connectedness between people, while men fear becoming entrapped in these very webs of interconnection (1982). Administrative organizational charts reflect this "male" perspective by graphically showing us who is on top (and conversely who is at the bottom), thus concentrating on who has power over whom (Pearson, Shavlik, and Touchton 1989, p. 272)

The concept of visionary, participative leadership, an emerging leadership style, is extremely important to improved institutional morale in higher education. As

Bryman reports, participative leadership enhances job satisfaction among people with a strong drive for independence and self-direction (1992). Drucker, appearing to be one of the earlier postmodern leadership and management theorists, wrote, "The knowledge worker cannot be supervised closely or in detail. He can only be helped. But he must direct himself toward performance and contribution . . ." (1967, p. 4). Participative leadership, therefore, would seem to be the preference of faculty members — individuals who experience low levels of task structure and whose work is ego-involving — as well as academicians who move into administrative ranks within higher education institutions.

Organizational Contexts
Regardless of how organizations are viewed, most contemporary conceptions of organization assume that leadership emanates from the apex of a hierarchy. "Organizational theory since its inception has its basis in hierarchical structures with explicit or implicit leadership, formal or informal, combining a relationship between leaders and followers" (Levin 1995, p. 12). A prevalent framework for organizational leadership theories is the Four Frames of Reference developed by Bolman and Deal (1984). Earlier, Baldridge et al. described three of the four frames and referred to the models as: the Academic Bureaucracy, the University Collegium, and the University as a Political System (1977). Bergquist also has explored and evaluated Bolman and Deal's and Birnbaum's frames as applied to collegiate institutions (1992).

Bolman and Deal's (1984) four frames were reevaluated based on higher education organizations by Robert Birnbaum (1988). Birnbaum kept the essence of Bolman and Deal's four frames and added a fifth integrated frame of reference he named the cybernetic system. In *Making Sense of Administrative Leadership: The "L" Word in Higher Education*, by Bensimon, Neumann, and Birnbaum, a comprehensive description is provided for each of these frames (1989). The authors conclude that cultural and symbolic theories are the most compatible with academic institutions. Briefly, the frames of reference as described by the authors include:

- The Bureaucratic/Structural Frame: Centralized systems are developed for coordination and control to direct the

work of others. The leader has final authority and decisionmaking and often is seen as the "hero" at the top of a
hierarchy. The institution is a relatively closed system
with an emphasis on rationality and performance. This
perspective focuses on the administrative role of the
leader who is viewed to be decisive, results-oriented, a
long-range planner, and a rational problem solver.

- The Collegium/Human Resource Frame: The institution is
considered to be a community of equals and differences
in status are deemphasized. In an environment that
stresses consensus, shared power, and participation in
governance, the leader is considered to be "the first
among equals" who serves the interests of group members. Attention is focused on the psychological aspects of
organizational life. The collegial culture relies on tradition and informal power. An authority mode is replaced
with consensus building and consultation.

- The Political Frame: Leaders mediate and negotiate between the shifting political groups, and the leader's
power is based on control of information and manipula-
tion of expertise. This perspective views the leader as a
"catalyst" who relies on diplomacy and persuasion to
build support for objectives that were developed through
a political process dominated by a negotiating culture.
Collegial or bureaucratic institutions that become large
and complex tend to evolve into political institutions.

- The Organized Anarchy/Symbolic Frame: The leader is
seen as a "facilitator" who brings a sense of organizational
purpose and reinforces institutional culture within an
ongoing process. The emphasis is on rituals, symbols,
stories, and the role of the organization. Virtually all ele-
ments of the institution are loosely coupled, thereby creating more of a community and less of an organization.
Leaders also negotiate with their positional influence.
"Garbage cans" provide outlets for unrelated and unre-
solved problems for institutional members. This perspective focuses on the role of the leader as a "guardian" of
the institution who utilizes intuition and symbolic interaction while managing the "garbage cans" of various interest groups.

- The Cybernetic System: This frame provides an overlap
among the Bureaucratic, Collegial, Symbolic, and Political
frames with consultation and communication processes as

the foundation. "Negative feedback loops" are created and reinforced to continually assess institutional performance. The monitors of these loops alert others if there is a problem or a critical area in the institution. Because of the role of the monitors, cybernetic institutions run themselves while leaders respond to disruptions and improve activities.

The framework under which the organization operates provides a cultural environment for its members. Institutional culture, as described by Masland, establishes a set of expectations and norms through purpose, commitment, and order (1985). The strength of a culture depends upon the size of the institution, the autonomy of the unit, the age of the institution, and the stage (birth or transformation) of its development.

"In colleges with stronger cultures, there is a greater coherence among beliefs, language, ritual, and myth" (Masland 1985, p. 159). The senior faculty often are the key group of believers who organize to protect the "legend" of the institution against later leaders and participants (Clark 1971). Organizational culture affects curriculum and administration in that resources are allocated based on the values of the institution (Kuh et al. 1991; Mintzberg 1989; Masland 1985). Articulated vs. enacted goals often are a function of cultural priorities shown through the allocation of resources by the institution (Mintzberg 1989).

It is the culture that personifies the institution's understood goals. In turn, the leader articulates the vision (Wilcox and Ebbs 1992; Roueche, Baker, and Rose 1989; O'Banion 1989; Cohen and Brawer 1982; Gleazer 1980) and manages the meaning (Bennis 1991; Smircich 1983) for the institution. Vision is amplified through institutional behavior, and meaning is shown through its culture. In essence, with a focus on diversity, financial constraint, and participatory management, the term "transformational leadership" is becoming synonymous with cultural management of higher education institutions.

Institutional culture, although often invisible to its members, provides a source of consistency and security for its members through shared values and assumptions. Deeply held assumptions often start out as values and are shown through institutional artifacts (Schein 1990). However, cul-

Institutional culture, as described by Masland, establishes a set of expectations and norms through purpose, commitment, and order.

ture evolves as members assert what values they deem to be most important (Kuh et al. 1991). As the culture evolves, so too does the operating philosophy of the institution.

Postmodern theorists agree with the need for ongoing cultural management, for they view successful organizations as continually changing to maintain equilibrium with external societal changes (Miller 1995). Academe, however, as shown by current data, has moved very slowly in the adoption of diverse leadership, and therefore diverse cultural environments, in higher education institutions. It is almost as if academe has developed an isolationist view — that is, not changing to maintain equilibrium with external society but rather holding on to old norms to inform current behavior and culture. As early as 1967, Peter Drucker discussed the need for organizations to change. He states, "An organization which just perpetuates today's level of vision, excellence, and accomplishment has lost the capacity to adapt. And since the one and only thing certain in human affairs is change, it will not be capable of survival in a changed tomorrow" (p. 57).

Traditional scholars of higher education leadership view the organization as a pyramid with the leader at the pinnacle (a power over position) and vast layers of members creating the structure over which she or he leads (Birnbaum 1989; Cohen and Brawer 1982; Gleazer 1980). Scholars and practitioners who have established discourse regarding the new voice of leadership, an emerging leadership mode, view the organization as a circle, with the leader(s) in the center of the web of relationships and activities (Helgesen 1995, 1990; Peters 1994; Blackmore and Kenway 1993; Garfield 1992; Wilkerson 1989). This circular view, a web of inclusion, focuses on collaboration, consensus, empowerment, and relationships (Covey 1991; Desjardins 1989; Gilligan 1982) as part of the leadership mode (Wilcox and Ebbs 1992; Wall et al. 1992; Senge 1990; Desjardins 1989) and institutional culture.

Bennis points to four themes evident if leadership is effective in empowering the workforce: (1) People feel significant; (2) learning and competence matter; (3) people are part of a community; and (4) work is exciting and challenging (1991). Stephen Covey's conditions of effectiveness and empowerment suggest that authoritarian leadership styles come from false assumptions about human nature, and these assumptions decrease motivation for peak performance

(1991). Helpful organizational systems develop self-directing, self-controlling individuals who in turn benefit the organization with increased effectiveness. Covey's six conditions of empowerment include communication, mutual agreements, self-supervision, and helpful structures and systems. Peters states that powerlessness vs. empowerment of employees is based on trust and, for organizations that need to make cultural changes, trust is the issue of the decade (1994).

The system in place informs internal members about institutional practices and decisionmaking processes. An autocratic, bureaucratic, political, or rational approach that dominates an institution implies that a hierarchical pyramid is in place. A symbolic approach can be based on political motives but also can be the result of cultural artifacts carried forward as part of the institutional history. The symbolic organization ultimately is hierarchical but has the appearance of being collaborative.

A collegial approach implies that the organization may have a horizontal leadership mode or may have several circles and power centers in a shared governance model. A collegial mode without conflict may indicate empowerment (power to members) but also may indicate a dominant majority rule (power over members) in which members are coerced into silence. The emerging posthierarchical approach encompasses a model that is circular, collaborative, and participatory and results in empowerment for members.

Individual Characteristics
Although it is difficult to define how charisma is personified in a leader, this notion is quite seductive and is conceptually appealing. Bryman states that ". . . since a charismatic leader who is bereft of a mission or vision is almost inconceivable, it is difficult to see how this element should be excluded from any conception of charisma which views the phenomenon [of leadership] as a social relationship" (1992, p. 41). Although charismatic leaders may be viewed as special or extraordinary, Bryman posits this view is fashioned more from the creation of myths and legends and the utilization of oratorical devices by the individual rather than from specific personal traits or physical characteristics. In other words, trait theory does not explain leadership — and particularly not charismatic leaders. "Traits alone are not sufficient to lead effectively. A leader must also behave in cer-

tain ways and possess key skills" (DuBrin 1994, p. 271).
Leaders utilize a host of influence tactics to accomplish their
goals. These include: leading by example, assertiveness,
rationality, ingratiation, exchange, and joking and kidding
(DuBrin 1994).

Drucker states that there are four basic requirements for
effective human relations by a CEO (1967). They are: com-
munications, teamwork, self-development, and development
of others. Warren Bennis describes four leadership competencies that draw people to a leader: (1) Leaders manage
attention through a vision that brings others to a new place;
(2) leaders make ideas tangible and real to others and garner
their support; (3) leaders have constancy and reliability and
therefore bring a sense of trust for others; and (4) leaders
know their skills and strengths and nurture them (1991).
Henry Mintzberg provides a list of needed leadership skills
that includes the ability to establish and maintain relationships, the ability to successfully mediate conflict and distur-
bances, the ability to disseminate information effectively, and
the ability to understand the impact of a leader upon an organization (1989). Mintzberg also states that leadership ultimately is political and that politics is the exercise of power.

Robert Birnbaum challenges both Bennis and Mintzberg's
interpretations of leadership, especially as they apply to
higher education institutions. Birnbaum posits that most
presidents would have to be satisfied knowing their role is
as a coordinator of a complex institution (1988, 1989).
Although Bennis and Mintzberg list competencies, skills, and
abilities leaders should acquire, Birnbaum claims that the
person in the position is irrelevant. The office is symboli-
cally rather than functionally important.

Further, Birnbaum indicates the need for presidents to
accumulate power for reciprocal relationships with institutional members (a social exchange theory) (1988).
Ultimately, he states, all presidents are similar in their impact
upon the institution. Birnbaum also indicates that most
presidents are similar in training, socialization, and characteristics and therefore appears to assume a homogeneous
population holds and will continue to hold presidential positions. This conclusion seems to forward the notion that
diversity has little to do with leadership perspectives and
that efforts at diversifying higher education leadership would
yield no change in institutional climate or culture.

Wilcox and Ebbs, however, view the president's position as having high impact upon the institution (1992). It is their contention that as a leader, the president is accountable for all that happens within an institution, academically as well as ethically. Further, they state that the classic hierarchical leadership role college and university presidents traditionally have adopted needs to be replaced with an ethos of community built through collaboration and shared governance. The authors discuss the care/connection voice through the moral reasoning (cognitive development theory) research of Carol Gilligan and the preference for relationship building in this mode (1982).

> *The implications of these distinctions are important; it could be possible that most college teaching, educational policies, and student-affairs programs favor one way of knowing over another. Care-voiced individuals, for example, seem to prefer collaborative discussion instead of competition and learning by listening to each other, rather than classes structured around dominance and subordination* (p. 47).

Wilcox and Ebbs explored the potential impact of the care/connection (response mode) and justice/rights (rights mode) voices upon leadership throughout the institution. They interpret the care/connection voice (response mode) in leadership to mean that decisionmaking in a collaborative environment is conducive to high morale and a sense of community within the institution. Although they note that all men and women use both voices, women have a preference for the care voice, whereas men prefer the justice voice. Their conclusion is that a high-impact, care-voiced leader could provide the institution with new values and ethics grounded in cooperation, community, and relationships within the community.

Carolyn Desjardins (1989) also utilizes Gilligan's (1982) coding system to analyze if gender determines leadership modes for community college CEOs. Desjardins' coding system defines the care/connection mode (mostly ascribed to females) as most concerned with the inner atmosphere, process, and relationships, while the justice/rights mode (mostly ascribed to males) focuses on outcomes, autonomy, and how the external community views the college.

Although all people have behaviors in both modes, they most often will respond out of one mode over the other. Sixty-six percent of women CEOs were found to be dominant in the care/connection mode, while 50 percent of male CEOs were dominant in the justice-rights mode (Desjardins 1989). She concludes that the care/connection (response) mode is more reflective of current trends toward participatory leadership but cautions that the care/connection mode might be more reflective of "people that are attracted to educational institutions" (p. 9).

Social constructionists (for example, Acker 1991; West and Zimmerman 1991; Gutek 1989; Burton 1987) would argue that the characteristics of the care/connection (response) mode, highly ascribed to women, are the result of societal expectations based on women's role in society and are not the result of actively pursued or achieved behaviors. This position is somewhat reflective of the traditional trait-theory argument that presumes superior ascribed characteristics of the "great man" as a leader. Trait theory assumes an individual is born with certain attributes that make him or her an effective leader but, as stated earlier in this report, traits alone are not sufficient to lead effectively.

Women's Leadership and the Leadership Frames
A review of leadership literature (for example, Bergquist 1992; Fryer and Lovas 1991; Bennis 1991; Bensimon, Neumann, and Birnbaum 1989; Roueche, Baker, and Rose 1989; Birnbaum 1988; Bolman and Deal 1984) reveals a strong leaning toward the Bureaucratic Frame as the operational preference for higher education institutions. Yet, most of these authors also voice a desire for visionary (political or symbolic) leadership and shared governance (collegium/human-resource frame) for the future. Those theorists who value institutional culture as a primary focus of analysis (Kuh et al. 1991; Masland 1985; Clark 1971) also speak to the symbolic frame. The symbolic, political, and human-resource frames, therefore, are considered to be usable models for an institution that is pursuing visionary goals and shared governance within its leadership model.

Although the voices of women can accommodate for traditional leadership theories and models, those voices do not parallel the traditional institutional culture in the academy. This asymmetry results in the nonacceptance of women in leadership roles within an organizational culture where male-dominated norms exist. When reviewing literature regarding leadership, whether within corporations or higher education, it can be readily discerned that current leadership theorists encourage a model that encompasses strong human-relations skills, a humanistic approach, collegiality, and consensus building (Levin 1994; Bergquist 1992; Wilcox and Ebbs 1992; Bennis 1991; Deegan, Tillery, and Associates 1991; Fryer 1991; Roueche, Baker, and Rose 1989). Tom Peters and Peter Drucker have made their preference for this model explicit in their current writings (Auburdene and Naisbitt 1992), as has Charles Garfield (1992). A sixth frame of reference, the web of inclusion (Helgesen 1995), emerges as a new, posthierarchical model for organizations. Peters states, "The lumbering bureaucracies of this century will be replaced with fluid, interdependent groups of problem solvers" but warns that this can be accomplished only when a true posthierarchical organization is the result of a cultural change (1994, p. 15). Senge's fifth discipline focuses on the development of learning organizations that are decentralized, nonhierarchical, and dedicated to the well-being and growth of employees (1990).

When cross-referencing postmodern, nonhierarchical leadership theories and models with gender-related research and scholarship, it becomes evident that the gender-related characteristics, described as innate to most women, encompass the very characteristics leadership theorists claim to be the most effective.

When viewing the leadership frames of reference through emerging, postmodern, or feminized leadership theory, it is even more difficult to determine why academe so hesitantly has included women in positions as CEO. The literature suggests that women, more than men, exhibit the relational characteristics encompassed within the three collaborative frames of leadership. In these terms, gender would be quite relevant for successful leadership as defined by several of the more current scholars in this field of study.

Perhaps one reason for the hesitancy are assumptions regarding the level of outcomes and length of time for the production of tangible results. According to the literature regarding men and women's leadership styles, women tend to be more focused on process, often forgoing time limitations to achieve collaborative processes, whereas men opt for quicker tangible outcomes through a focus on tasks and time lines (Kearny and White 1994; Desjardins 1989). Although the ultimate tangible results may be the same (but most authors of emerging leadership literature suggest the results would be significantly different), speed may be the determining factor by which leader effectiveness is evaluated. Therefore, speed and not process may determine who is considered "effective" as a leader.

A collaborative institutional system, a collegium, often espoused as being of prime importance in higher education, may never occur if effectiveness is measured by time rather than full participation. With this type of evaluation criterion, collaborative, collegial systems consistently may lose out to autocratic and bureaucratic systems, slowing progress toward the attainment of equitable and diverse leadership in higher education.

Summarizing Individual, Organizational, and Societal Conceptualizations

Most contemporary conceptions of organizations assume a hierarchical structure with leadership emanating from the apex of the hierarchy. However, a nonbureaucratic form of leadership is forwarded by emerging and feminist theorists as a more egalitarian social system. The choice of organizational structure is critical to the framework under which the organization operates, for the framework provides a cultural environment and social structure for its members.

Organizational culture establishes a set of expectations and norms which in turn affect the allocation of resources within the institution. Culture personifies the institution's understood goals while the leader articulates the vision and manages the meaning for the institution. Further, the empowerment or disenfranchisement of institutional members becomes embedded within the framework of the organization's culture, structure, and allocation of resources.

Conceptions of the impact of individuals who hold leadership positions varies among scholars. Some view leadership as symbolic and low-impact, whereas others view leadership as highly related to conceptions of shared governance and an ethos of community within the institution. In particular, several scholars and researchers have indicated that participatory leadership is related more to women's leadership style then to men's (for example, Helgesen 1995, 1990; Desjardins 1989). Most prevalent in these writings are conceptualizations of differences in power and power relations based on gender. In turn, these differences culminate in perspectives that counter traditional leadership notions.

For example, even though recent scholarship on higher education leadership touts collaborative institutional systems as being of primary importance, traditional evaluation criteria continue to view outcomes-oriented leadership as superior to process-oriented leadership. That is, there is an expectation that a leader will "make things happen" rather than facilitate a process for institutional changes to occur; member participation becomes secondary to institutional outcomes.

The complex structure of organizations creates concepts of organizational roles and images of the kinds of people who should occupy them. Although in the abstract those images are gender-neutral, the crowding of women in the lower ranks of organizations implies there are gendered images of men and women's roles in organizations. As Senge points out, "Structures of which we are unaware hold us prisoner" (1990, p. 94). Thus, postmodernists have identified socially constructed role ascriptions based on gender rather than ability as the basis for leadership conceptualizations. Furthermore, gender-role theorists take to task those who assume that sameness means equality. Ideal images of successful leadership, which are equated with male behaviors, need to be replaced with images of human ability within diverse organizational structures and cultures. These issues are attended to through rules of inclusion and exclusion within discourse about leadership.

FACTORS INFLUENCING EVALUATIONS
OF LEADERS AND LEADERSHIP MODES

An individual may be an *emergent* leader, assuming a leadership role though group consensus, or the leader may be *appointed*, as by the board of a university. So, regardless of whether a woman is an *emergent* leader or an *appointed* leader, what happens during the evaluation process? Is she perceived to lead as well as a man? And, will people respond positively to her leadership?

Evaluating Women as Leaders

A 1992 meta-analysis (Eagly, Makhijani, and Klonsky) of gender and the evaluation of leaders found that the empirical literature addressing the issue of whether women are devalued in leadership roles, regardless of organization or occupation, is substantial although divergent in their opinions. The authors based their predications on gender-role theory that maintains that "people develop expectations for their own and other's behavior based on their beliefs about the behavior that is appropriate for men and women" (1992, p. 5).

Women leaders were evaluated more negatively than were men when exhibiting autocratic behavior.

Women leaders were evaluated more negatively than were men when exhibiting autocratic behavior. The researchers noted that experts on leader effectiveness have criticized the hierarchical and rigid bureaucratic forms of organizations and traditional management practices for this negative effect. Through prior research, for example, they found a tendency for female leaders to be especially devalued when they direct male subordinates.

Conclusions of Eagly, Makhijani, and Klonsky's meta-analysis support the notion that traditional masculine leadership styles (autocratic, directive) are seen as more favorable for male leaders and cooperative, collaborative and collegial work environments are more likely through women's participative leadership styles. They also note that the participative style is less prevalent among men. Johnson, in researching gender and authority, found that male and female leaders were perceived as being similar in their positive socioemotional demeanor; however, employees perceived female leaders as more task-oriented than male leaders (1993). Johnson defers to Eagly's findings as an explanation. Whereas women are viewed as more extreme and less in keeping with traditional female/feminine stereotypes, their behavior actually may be identical to that of their male cohorts (Johnson 1993).

Schaef describes tactics utilized in patriarchal systems which are both negatively evaluative of women and "stoppers" for "deviant" behavior so that order can be restored to the organizational universe (1985). By coworkers implying that a woman is aggressive or close-minded, the woman is put in a one-down position professionally and organizationally. "Men who stand up for themselves are competent and assertive; women who do the same are obnoxious and aggressive. Men who openly express different opinions to women are forthright and honest; women who do the same [to men] are castrating bitches who have no regard for the fragile male ego" (p. 74).

The meta-analysis findings support the hypothesis that women are negatively evaluated when exhibiting masculine leadership styles while men and women are evaluated equivalently when leadership is carried out in more stereotypical styles (for example, democratic and interpersonally oriented for women). The Center for Values and Research in Dallas similarly concludes in a study that coworkers are more negative toward women managers then men managers who lack human-relations skills and/or are seen as aggressive (Aburdene and Naisbitt 1992). Women managers in Sheppard's (1992) and Milwid's (1990) studies attempted not to challenge the prevailing sex norms and developed strategies to combat isolation and perceived double standards in their management roles.

Although Kelly discusses the difficulty in exploring behavioral styles, her research results indicate an impact of sex on administrative style and success (1991). Kelly states, "We know that behaviors such as aggressiveness, competitiveness, and dominance receive different reactions depending upon the sex of the actor. Behavior that is perceived as 'bitchiness' in women is often perceived as gruffness or acceptable aggressiveness in men" (p. 107). Further, her findings suggest no significant gender differences exist in administrative aptitude, although the perception is that there are gender differences in behavioral styles which then result in differences in evaluations.

Who Has the Right to Leadership Positions?
Differentiation in leadership modes and evaluations of who has the "right" to leadership begin early in a child's life and follow into adulthood. Evaluations of the individual as a leader are based on expected and learned gender-related patterns and norms. Girls learn that other girls evaluate

behaviors other than sharing and consensus building as being "bossy"; boys learn that if they do not exert influence they are considered "wimps" (Tannen 1994).

Boys and girls, while in school, engage in a "cootie game" in which, for the most part, it is girls who have cooties and girls as a group are treated as an ultimate source of contamination (Thorne 1994). Boys define hierarchies and often use the label of "girl" for the low-status boys, physically pushing these boys into the girls' contaminated area. "Recoiling from the physical proximity with another person because they are perceived as contaminating is a powerful statement of social distance and claimed superiority" (p. 75).

The seemingly normal games of childhood become learned messages about the value and rights of other human beings. In this case, girls with "cooties" become women who contaminate work sites and therefore have a negative value in the workplace. Several researchers provide evidence that even when women do the same work as men, they are not perceived as being as competent as men nor is their work perceived to be as prestigious (Kelly 1991; Reskin and Roos 1990; Freeman 1989).

Summarizing Evaluations of Leaders

In summary, women and men leaders are evaluated differently based on the way they conduct their leadership rather than on their effectiveness as a leader. In particular, women are devalued when they direct male subordinates and when they exhibit autocratic or directive behavior. And, although participative leadership is less prevalent among men, the adoption of a participative style or an autocratic style makes little difference in men's leadership evaluations.

Evaluations of individuals as leaders appear to be based more on expected gender-related patterns and norms than on managerial aptitude or socioemotional demeanor. Furthermore, regardless of ability or effort, evidence suggests that even when work is performed in positions and ways similar to those of men, women are not perceived as competent as men nor is the position considered as prestigious.

CONCLUSIONS, IMPLICATIONS, AND RECOMMENDATIONS

Conclusions

Regardless of the scholar or the perspective from which she or he writes, leadership is needed in an institution. Whether it is the "great man" who leads at the head of a hierarchy or through a consensus mode in a network, leadership is an integral part of a functioning institution. "Although several disciplines have debunked the great man or great person theory of leadership, this concept is still prevalent in higher education scholarship and practice" (Mott 1997) and cannot be denied as a factor in the perpetuation of selecting male candidates for higher education leadership positions.

Amey and Twombly, for example, deconstructed the language of community college literature and found the "great man" to be a prevalent feature (1992); Roueche, Baker, and Rose described "blue chip" community college leaders, only 10 percent of whom were women (1989); and Mitchell in *Cracking the Wall* suggests androgyny as a solution for women to combat the difficulties associated with their gender when attempting to attain higher education administrative positions (1993).

When putting leadership in context, a question raised is whether the leader leads or follows a culture that already has been established. This question, however, is raised when the leader is viewed as being part of a pyramid structure; a circular form of leadership does not have followers, it has participatory members. And, according to Miller and Hurley, "In the final analysis only followers can confer leadership based upon a trust relationship carefully cultivated and nurtured . . ." (1985, p. 2).

Amey and Twombly utilize discourse analysis to decipher historical and current perspectives on college leadership (1992). Through their analysis, they find a thematic structure of text and talk that implies images of a heroic white male as the decisive and powerful leader of an institution. Their analysis is based on sociohistorical and organizational life cycles of the community college, and they find "these images have been consistent in community college literature over time" (p. 141) and further, "Alternative voices and images of leadership, while not exclusively those of women, have most frequently emerged from the feminist movement" (p. 143). Unlike mainstream authors and observers of higher education, emerging voices promote leadership based on connectedness and collaboration rather than traditional views of hierarchy, authority, and power.

The current status of feminist scholarship, though deemed "second-class" scholarship in the academy, has not enjoyed a broad audience and often is excluded by the professorate as well as higher education's administrative ranks (Wilson 1997; MacCorquodale and Linsink 1991; Gumport 1988, 1991). The aversion to feminist scholarship, unfortunately, leaves members of the academy uninformed as well as misinformed.

The essence of the problem regarding the gender gap in higher education institutional culture, as expressed by many writers who discuss the issues of gender and marginalizing of classes of people, is that certain ideas simply are excluded through cultural norming (Lefkowitz 1994; Kuk 1990; Smith 1990; Pearson, Shavlik, and Touchton 1989; Wilkerson 1989; Fox 1989) and through the lack of diversity in faculty makeup and in those who hold institutional leadership positions (Johnsrud 1994; Wilcox and Ebbs 1992; Hensel 1991; Green 1989; Desjardins 1989).

As a historically patriarchal institution, academe continues to perpetuate a normed male hierarchy that indicates men's inclusion and women's exclusion. Minority-group members also feel a chill from the gatekeepers of the status quo. The accumulation of merit and the "right" to hold a leadership position more often is believed to be a process of sacrifice rather than a system of inclusion by those who continue to be marginalized. However, the power of institutional gatekeepers is assuring to traditionally socialized members in higher education institutions who believe that reproduction of the status quo is a legitimate institutional goal.

The emerging leadership model attends to human issues of participatory management, consensus building, collaboration, and empowerment. Relationship building, circular structures, an inclusionary process, and concern with the inner social atmosphere and culture of the institution are described as being functions of individuals who operate from the care/connection (response) mode; a mode more ascribed to women than men. For the purpose of analyzing leadership theory, questions about whether a difference exists between males and females and the care/connection (response) mode and the justice/rights (rights) mode become quite relevant. These differences potentially could address whether there would be significant institutional improvements if women, and an emerging posthierarchical or feminized leadership style, were more prevalent in higher education.

Implications

Leadership deals with direction and management deals with speed; leadership deals with the top line, management focuses on the bottom line (Covey 1991). If there is no leader, there is also a lack of vision and mission. Without leadership, ambiguity overtakes the organization. Covey points to one of the major problems in historically and culturally traditional institutions such as higher education. "It seems that people tend to codify past successful practices into rules for the future and give energy to preserving and enforcing these rules even after they no longer apply" (p. 245). Thus, any powerful culture dies hard.

Traditional academic culture informs its members that meritocratic criteria is structured to allow for "cream to rise to the top." This same structure implies that traditional, not emerging, voices will receive deference in a meritocratic system, as is shown through such practices as tenure-track criteria, the marginalizing of certain studies, and the clustering of women in certain ranks and occupations. Senge explains that systematic structures are concerned with key interrelationships that influence behavior over time, and participants within these structures are compelled to act and think in certain ways (1990). Institutionalized patriarchy, based on socialization and cultural norms, envisions a zero-sum game whereby a gain in emerging theory means a loss in traditional theory; a gain in diversification of leadership means a loss in traditional leadership. For some members of academe, this has posed quite a dilemma.

Working from the assumption that women have a different voice and therefore a different mode of leadership, we need to move forward to determine how this difference brings a new and positive value and can become incorporated and accepted in our current social and cultural systems. The change potentially could impact models and modes in classrooms, boardrooms, and scholarship, thereby reducing claims of chilly campus climate and exclusionary practices. Men also would feel some relief with the implementation of these changes for, as noted throughout this

Institutionalized patriarchy, based on socialization and cultural norms, envisions a zero-sum game whereby a gain in emerging theory means a loss in traditional theory; a gain in diversification of leadership means a loss in traditional leadership.

report, the response mode and rights mode are gender-related, not gender-specific. Many men, whether traditionally oriented or feminists, also would have the freedom to perform their leadership role in a mode with which they are more comfortable, rather than a mode perceived to be typically masculine.

Research on leadership, and in particular research on leaders as change agents, shows that change is possible within most institutions. Although the culture of academe seemingly is steeped in a traditionally male dominant set of norms, it is not impossible to pursue a change process.

It is not the time to refrain from pushing forward with more questions regarding leadership diversity, an emerging theory of leadership, and conceptualizations of gendered voices. Gender-related issues and concerns in academe are being articulated more clearly than ever before. Only when there are "new visions of an academic order emphasizing empowerment and relatedness while minimizing dominance, competition, and hierarchy" will there be a full acceptance of women's voices and feminized leadership in higher education (Gumport 1988).

Recommendations

The barriers to feminized leadership need to be broken down carefully and successfully. Strongly dominated by men (eight of 10 university and college presidents are male; almost nine of every 10 chief business officers are male; and seven of 10 chief academic officers are male), current leadership is not reflective of the nation's student body (more than half of the student enrollment is female). When leadership positions become less elusive for women and a critical mass of women accrues in all areas of higher education, cultural norms within male-dominated institutions might become more open to challenges for shared governance, member empowerment, and decisionmaking through a process of consensus. Following are recommended strategies for change:

1. It is easier to promote change when you are in a position which establishes institutional vision, norms, and forms. Women who move from institutional caretaker to gatekeeper positions can influence other gatekeepers to become involved in transforming hierarchical and/or

patriarchal structures and norms (Blackmore and Kenway 1993; Amey and Twombly 1992). Transformational leadership develops consensus and empowers those who are sympathetic to a goal and, in turn, those who are empowered provide models of success to validate and encourage changes for others.

Once cumulative, incremental changes can be extremely effective (Pearson, Touchton, and Shavlik 1989). Women who hold senior-level positions are especially obligated to assist other women who aspire to leadership roles and to redefine acceptable institutional policies and practices (Tinsley, Secor, and Kaplan 1984). Further, since "patriarchy is organized through men's relationships with other men, unity among women . . ." is an effective means by which to combat institutionalized forms of exclusion for women (Anderson 1988, p. 323). If hierarchical organizations are the result of masculine concepts, nonhierarchical forms require cultural change based on women's relationships with like-minded women and men.

2. If anyone wants to change culture, it is easier to do in institutions that are small, new, or being transformed (Masland 1985). Women already are taking steps in this area for, as the data show, 71 percent of women presidents are in institutions with 3,000 or less students (Rigaux 1995). Further, taking a new or beginning leadership position in an autonomous part of a larger system would provide for more leadership prowess rather than when part of a highly interdependent department, often overseen by the male hierarchy.

Women who desire broader responsibilities in larger institutions need to be prepared to relocate if an opportunity arises. Research has shown this to be a difficult situation for women who are married. Career mobility often is stifled by familial rather than geographic limitations. Just as women have had to do in the past, married men who support women's aspirations and women's equality must objectively weigh their commitment to their own career in relationship to their commitment to a partner's aspirations and career.

3. The transformational leader is one who embodies the ideals and cultural values toward which the organization

strives (Garfield 1992; Bryman 1992; Covey 1991).
Transformational-leadership behaviors (those which
encompass organizational-change behaviors rather than
management behaviors) need to be promoted and developed by women. Basic, rote management skills,
although functionally useful in bureaucratic systems, are
not the skills that provide empowerment for members
or visionary leadership by the CEO. Bryman explains
that managers tend to be more practical and decisive,
while leaders tend to be more visionary and flexible
(1992). Also, leaders establish the vision, whereas managers are concerned with implementing the vision.

4. Regardless of position, women in higher education must
   eliminate the sense of being a marginal member or an
   unequal member of the academy. This debilitating position leaves women with a feeling of gratitude to the
   "benevolent patriarch" when equal pay or recognition is
   given for a job well done (Blackmore and Kenway
   1993). For example, morally we know that the wage
   gap is unfair. Yet, this practice maintains a pecking
   order that implies hierarchical institutional value and
   respect for members, regardless of equal contribution.
   A posthierarchical organization, however, is compelled
   to promote the legitimate and equal positioning of
   women in the economics of the organization.

5. Eliminating campuswide micro-inequities, those behaviors and actions that create a chilly campus climate for
   women and minority groups, is a major step in bringing
   full equity to half of the campus population (Henry and
   Stockdale 1995; Sandler and Hall 1982, 1986). Until men
   and women respect and value each other as professionals and students and until faculty members fully participate in inclusionary pedagogy, women's places in the
   academy will not become part of a fully integrated social system. (See MacCorquodale and Lensink 1991 for
   results of a pedagogical project conducted at a Research
   One university.)

6. The data would indicate that higher education generally
   maintains an occupationally segregated workforce, the
   result of the persistence factors discussed. With the

inequity of numbers, should there be a concerted effort to place females into leadership positions? Cries of "foul!" surely would arise if this path was taken. Equal rights ultimately means equal opportunity — regardless of gender, ethnicity, race, or personal lifestyle preferences.

What cannot go unstated in this debate, however, is that rights have not always been equal; preferential treatment, as evidenced by the data, has been in place for many decades. Tipping the scale on the side of decisions based on gender or race/ethnicity, assuming that the candidates are equal in all other respects, ultimately would provide for treatment that finally is equally dispensed. England provides guidance for determining an occupationally segregated workforce (1992). With slightly more than 40 percent of the labor force comprising women, integrated occupations would have approximately 30 to 50 percent female incumbents. Higher education leadership is barely halfway to meeting the minimum for this integration standard.

An interview with Georgia Lesh-Laurie, vice chancellor at the University of Colorado at Denver, provides a woman's perspective on selection based on gender (Westerhof 1995). She says, "I know that gender played a role in my appointment . . ." but, instead of apologizing for getting into administration through the side door of affirmative action, she states that her goal "is to be the best academic vice chancellor" who could have been selected. A highly motivated leader who wants to prove the worth of her selection certainly is an asset for any institution. Additionally, as is evident through research, because of the microscope under which women are scrutinized in the workplace they tend to work harder and longer than their male counterparts in similar positions.

What cannot go unstated in this debate, however, is that rights have not always been equal; preferential treatment, as evidenced by the data, has been in place for many decades.

7. Institutional culture is a function of an institution's goals and actions and the leader's management of a vision. Affirmative action (or diversity action) is important to universities in that a pluralistic community is more welcoming to all its members. However, the success of affirmative action depends on leaders and boards who are willing to make this issue part of their institutional

agenda. With clearly stated institutional goals at the onset, any institutional changes that include diversity or plurality as part of a plan of implementation would be shown to be part of a normal diversification process.

Regardless of whether an institution seeks to fill a position or consider a change in policy, a concern with diversification would be a known and articulated issue. When an issue is considered "convenient" or "seldom used" or brought to the forefront in the middle of process, a hue and cry is raised. As stated elsewhere in this report, institutional culture is a socially constructed phenomenon that can be constructed to be inclusive or exclusionary. Opting for a culture that is inclusive establishes a set of cultural norms that eventually become part of the members' understanding of the institution's functioning.

8. Studies of gender differences and women's communication modes indicate weaknesses as well as strengths related to women's way of knowing. Women can continue to be both active creators and passive victims in their environments based on what they choose to ignore or adopt as feminized practices (Ferguson 1984).

Although gender differences may be potentially important in redefining leadership, Gilligan's research indicates that women's cognitive development has a possible negative effect for women — the tendency to be "nice" to others at the expense of being self-appreciating and/or confrontal depending upon the situation. Niceness, while avoiding hurting other people's feelings, becomes an enabling tool for others to continue their old habits, behaviors, and adherence to established norms and values. Women need to make a concerted effort to recognize the difference between concession and negotiation, the first of which usurps leadership potential and the second which builds institutional relationships and member empowerment.

10. To better understand reasons for the slow integration of women into academe's leadership ranks and to push forward with women's' integration, directions for future research could include:

- Conduct comparisons of female- and male-led institutions in higher education, particularly focusing on governance processes and institutional initiatives. These studies are beginning to occur with female CEOs. Starr Owens has conducted a case study on a college in leadership transition (1993); Maxine Mott completed dissertation research focusing on determining whether female community college presidents incorporate a feminist perspective in their institutional agendas (1997).
- Study the composition of governing boards and the types of CEOs they hire. Do homogeneous boards hire people like themselves and/or do boards that are diverse in composition hire a broader range of CEOs?
- A study of higher education leadership-evaluation criteria to determine if process-oriented leaders are devalued and/or if outcomes are the primary evaluation criterion by institutional members. Chliwniak's 1996 study indicates this is a factor in leadership-evaluation perceptions of chancellors, presidents, provosts, vice presidents, and deans, and more so for women than men.
- Study the language of higher education leadership. Similar to Deborah Tannen's findings in the workplace, is there "doublespeak" internally and externally regarding women and men leaders?

A Final Note

It is important to remain aware of the possibility that many of the issues discussed in this report are a result of systems and not individuals (Schaef 1985; Kanter 1977). These systems control almost every aspect of organizational culture and the individuals within them. The clustering of women in the lower ranks, the wage gap, and the "riskiness" of a feminist academic vocation are the result of conservative, traditional cultures and systems. However, because they are only systems they can be examined and changed, with positive aspects maintained and negative or exclusionary practices terminated.

Further, of most importance in the process of change is that "equality cannot be externally assigned until it has been internally perceived" by institutional members (Schaef 1985, p. 74). That is, by attending to institutional practices such as tenure criteria, tenure tracks, pedagogy, marginalizing of studies dominated by women, sexual harassment, wage gaps, personal and career issues of women, and curriculum based on the generic male model, incremental but effective changes can reshape institutional culture. As changes are made in each of these practices, our mothers, daughters, and female friends or partners can become more equal members — and perhaps leaders — in the vast American system of higher education.

REFERENCES

Aburdene, P., and J. Naisbitt. 1992. *Megatrends for Women.* New York: Villard Books.

Acker, J. 1991. "Hierarchies, Jobs, Bodies: A Theory of Gendered Organization." In *The Social Construction of Gender.* Newbury Park, Calif.: Sage Publications.

Adams, K. January 1995. "Women in Community College Administration: A Study of Sex-Role Orientation and Job Satisfaction." In the proceedings of the Eighth Annual International Conference on Women in Higher Education. San Francisco.

Allen, R.F., J. Allen, B. Certner, and C. Kraft. 1988. *The Organizational Unconscious: How to Create the Corporate Culture You Want and Need.* Englewood Cliffs, N.J.: Prentice-Hall.

Alpern, D. July 1995. "Why Women are Divided on Affirmative Action." *Working Woman.*

Amey, M.J., and S.B. Twombly. Winter 1992. "Revisioning Leadership in Community Colleges." *The Review of Higher Education* 15(2): 125-50.

Anderson, M.L. 1988. *Thinking About Women: Sociological Perspectives on Sex and Gender.* 2nd ed. New York: Macmillan.

Astin, H.S., and D.E. Davis. 1985. "Research Productivity Across the Life and Career Cycles: Facilitators and Barriers for Women." In *Scholarly Writing and Publishing: Issues, Problems, and Solutions.* M. Fox, ed. Boulder, Colo.: Westview Press.

Aufderheid, P., ed. 1992. *Beyond PC: Toward a Politics of Understanding.* St. Paul, Minn.: Graywolf Press.

Baier, A.C. 1985. "What Do Women Want in a Moral Theory?" *Nous* 19(1): 53-63.

Baldridge, J., D. Curtis, G. Ecker, and G. Riley. 1988. "Alternative Models of Governance in Higher Education." In *Governing Academic Organizations.* Berkeley, Calif.: McCutchan Publishing Corp.

Bell, D. April 4, 1997. "Protecting Diversity Programs From Political and Judicial Attack." *Chronicle of Higher Education.*

Bellas, M. March 1993. "Faculty Salaries: Still a Cost of Being Female?" *Social Science Quarterly* 74(1).

Bengiveno, T.A. 1995. "Women and Education: Barriers to Self Fulfillment, Solutions to Inequality." In the proceedings of the Eighth Annual International Conference on Women in Higher Education. San Francisco.

Bennis, W. 1991. *Why Leaders Can't Lead: The Unconscious Conspiracy Continues.* San Francisco: Jossey-Bass.

Bensimon, E., A. Neumann, and R. Birnbaum. 1989. *Making Sense of Administrative Leadership: The "L" Word in Higher Education.*

ASHE-ERIC Higher Education Report No. 1. Washington, D.C.: The George Washington University, Graduate School of Education and Human Development. ED 316 074. 121 pp. MF-01; PC-05.

Bergquist, W. 1992. "Acknowledging Cultural Realities in Academic Leadership." In *The Four Cultures of the Academy: Insights and Strategies for Improving Leadership in Collegiate Organizations*. San Francisco: Jossey-Bass.

Berkowitz, P. January 1996. *More Alike Than Different: A Look at Male and Female Experiences in University Administration*. University affairs, Association of Universities and Colleges of Canada.

Birnbaum, R. 1989. "Responsibility Without Authority: The Impossible Job of the College President." In *Higher Education Handbook of Theory and Research*, vol. 5. J.C. Smart, ed. New York: Agathon Press.

———. March/April 1989. "Presidential Succession in Institutional Functioning in Higher Education." *Journal of Higher Education* 60(2). EJ 389 086.

Blackmore, J., and J. Kenway, eds. 1993. *Gender Matters in Educational Administration and Policy: A Feminist Introduction*. Washington, D.C.: Falmer Press.

Bolman, L., and T. Deal. 1984. *Modern Approaches to Understanding and Managing Organizations*. San Francisco: Jossey-Bass.

Brookover, W.B., and Associates. 1965. *The College Student*. New York: The Center for Applied Research in Education, Inc.

Brown, M., and W. Walworth. Winter 1985-86. "Educational Leadership: College Presidents in the Decade Ahead." *The College Board Review* (138).

Bruhn, J.G. 1993. "Administrators Who Cannot Let Go: The Super Manager Syndrome." *Health Care Supervisor* 11(3): 35-42.

Burton, C. 1987. "Merit and Gender: Organizations and the Mobilization of Masculine Bias." *Australian Journal of Social Issues* 22(2): 424-35.

Bryman, A. 1992. *Charisma and Leadership in Organizations*. Newbury Park, Calif.: Sage Publications.

Cage, M.C. January 26, 1994. "Beyond the B.A." *Chronicle of Higher Education* XL(21).

Chliwniak, L. 1995. "The Perpetuation of the Gender Gap in Higher Education Leadership." In the proceedings of the Eighth Annual International Conference on Women in Higher Education. San Francisco.

————. 1996. "Men and Women in Higher Education: Perceptions of Leadership Values and Modes." Ph.D. dissertation, University of Arizona.

Clark, B. 1972. "The Organizational Saga in Higher Education." *Administrative Science Quarterly* 17(2): 178-84.

Cohen, A., and F. Brawer. 1982. *The American Community College.* San Francisco: Jossey-Bass.

Covey, S.R. 1991. *Principle-Centered Leadership.* New York: Simon and Schuster.

Cuming, P. 1985. *Turf and Other Corporate Power Plays.* Englewood Cliffs, N.J.: Prentice-Hall.

Deegan, W., D. Tillery, and Associates, eds. 1991. *Renewing the American Community College.* San Francisco: Jossey-Bass.

Desjardins, C. 1989. "Gender Issues in Community College Leadership." *AAWCJC Journal:* 5-10.

Drucker, P.F. 1967. *The Effective Executive.* New York: Harper Business.

DuBrin, A.J. 1994. *Essentials of Management.* Cincinnati: South-Western Publishing Co.

Eagly, A.H., and B.T. Johnson. 1990. "Gender and Leadership Style: A Meta-Analysis." *Psychological Bulletin* 108(2): 233-56.

————, and S.J. Karau. 1991. "Gender and the Emergence of Leaders: A Meta-Analysis." *Journal of Personality and Social Psychology* 60(5): 685-710.

————, M.G. Makhijani, and B.G. Klonsky. 1992. "Gender and the Evaluation of Leaders: A Meta-Analysis." *Psychological Bulletin* I08(2): 3-22.

Edge, R., and J. Groves. 1994. *The Ethics of Health Care: A Guide for Clinical Practice.* Albany, N.Y.: Delmar Publishers.

Eichenbaum, L., and S. Orbach. 1982. *Outside In Inside Out: Women's Psychology: A Feminist Psychoanalytic Approach.* England: Penguin Books Ltd.

England, P. 1992. *Comparable Worth: Theories and Evidence.* New York: Aldine de Gruyter.

Faludi, S. 1991. *Backlash: The Undeclared War Against American Women.* New York: Doubleday.

Ferguson, K.E. 1984. *The Feminist Case Against Bureaucracy.* Philadelphia: Temple University Press.

Finkel, S.K., and S.G. Olswang. January 1995. "Childrearing, Sexism, and Sexual Harassment as Barriers to Tenure for Female Assistant Professors." In the proceedings of the Eighth Annual International Conference on Women in Higher Education. San Francisco.

Flynn, M.T. 1993. "Questioning the System: A Feminist Perspective." In *Cracking the Wall*. P.T. Mitchell, ed. Washington, D.C.: College and University Personnel Association.

Fox, M.F. 1989. "Women in Higher Education: Gender Differences in the Status of Students and Scholars." In *Women: A Feminist Perspective*. 4th ed. Mountain View, Calif.: Mayfield Publishing Co.

Freeman, J. 1989. *Women: A Feminist Perspective*. 4th ed. Mountain View, Calif.: Mayfield Publishing Co.

Fryer, T.W. Jr., and J.C. Lovas. 1991. "Successful Governance: What Really Matters." In *Leadership and Governance*. San Francisco: Jossey-Bass.

Gallimore-McKee, J. 1991. "Leadership Styles of Community College Presidents and Faculty Job Satisfaction." *Community/Junior College* 15: 33-46.

Garfield, C. 1992. *Second to None: How Our Smartest Companies Put People First*. Homewood, Ill.: Irwin Publishers.

Gilligan, C. 1982. *In a Different Voice: Psychological Theory and Women's Development*. Cambridge, Mass.: Harvard University Press.

Gilligan, C., J.V. Ward, and J.M. Taylor, eds. 1988. *Mapping the Moral Domain: A Contribution of Women's Thinking to Psychological Theory and Education*. Cambridge, Mass.: Harvard University Press.

Gleazer, E.J. Jr. 1980. "Leadership." In *The Community College: Values, Vision and Vitality*. Washington, D.C.: American Association of Community and Junior Colleges.

Gornick, V., and B. Moran, eds. 1971. *Women in Sexist Society: Studies in Power and Powerlessness*. New York: New American Library.

Green, M.F. 1989. *Minorities on Campus: A Handbook for Enhancing Diversity*. Washington, D.C.: American Council on Education.

Gumport, P.J. Autumn 1988. "Curricula as Signposts of Cultural Change." *The Review of Higher Education* 12(1): 49-61.

———. 1991. "Feminist Scholarship as a Vocation." In *Women's Higher Education in Comparative Perspective*. G.P. Kelly and S. Slaughter, eds. Netherlands: Kluwer Academic Publishers.

Gutek, B. 1989. "Sexuality in the Workplace: Key Issues in Social Research and Organizational Practice." In *The Sexuality of Organization*. Hearn, Sheppard, Tancred-Sheriff, and Burrell, eds. Newbury Park, Calif.: Sage Publications.

Hanna, C. July/August 1988. "The Organizational Context for

Affirmative Action for Women Faculty." *Journal of Higher Education* 59(4).

Hare-Mustin, R., and J. Marecek. June 1988. "The Meaning of Difference: Gender Theory, Postmodernism, and Psychology." *American Psychologist* 43(6).

Hartmann, H. 1976. "Capitalism, Patriarchy, and Job Segregation by Sex." *Signs: Journal of Women in Culture and Society, 1 (Part 2):* 137-69.

Haworth, J.G., and C. Conrad, eds. 1993. *Curriculum in Transition.* Needham Heights, Mass.: Ginn Publishers.

Helgesen, S. 1990. *The Female Advantage: Women's Ways of Leadership.* New York: Doubleday.

———. 1995. *The Web of Inclusion: A New Architecture for Building Great Organizations.* New York: Currency/Doubleday.

Henry, J., and M. Stockdale. January 1995. "The Climate for Conducting Climate Surveys." In the proceedings of the Eighth Annual International Conference on Women in Higher Education. San Francisco.

Hensel, N. 1991. *Realizing Gender Equality in Higher Education: The Need to Integrate Work/Family Issues.* ASHE-ERIC Higher Education Report No. 2. Washington, D.C.: Association for the Study of Higher Education. ED 338 128. 122 pp. MF-01; PC-05.

Jager, A., and P. Rothenberg. 1993. *Feminist Frameworks: Alternative Theoretical Accounts of the Relations Between Women and Men.* 3d ed. New York: McGraw Hill.

Johnson, C. 1993. "Gender and Formal Authority." *Social Psychology Quarterly* 56(3): 193-210.

Johnson, F.L. Summer 1993. "Women's Leadership in Higher Education: Is the Agenda Feminist?" *College and University Personnel Association Journal.*

Johnsrud, L.K., and R.H. Heck. January/February 1994. "Administrative Promotion With a University: The Cumulative Impact of Gender." *Journal of Higher Education* 65(1).

Kandyoti, D. 1989. "Bargaining with Patriarchy." In *The Social Construction of Gender.* Newbury Park, Calif.: Sage Publications.

Kanter, R.M. 1977. *Men and Women of the Corporation.* New York: Basic Books.

Katz, M., and V. Vieland. 1988. *Get Smart! A Woman's Guide to Equality on Campus.* New York: The Feminist Press at the City University of New York.

Kearney, K., and T. White. 1994. *Men and Women at Work.* Hawthorne, N.J.: Career Press.

Kelly, R.M. 1991. *The Gendered Economy: Work, Careers, and*

Success. Newbury Park, Calif.: Sage Publications.

Kirby, S., D. Daniels, K. McKenna, M. Pujol, M. Valiquette, eds. 1991. *Women Changing Academe: The Proceedings of the 1990 Canadian Women's Studies Association Conference.* Winnipeg, Canada: Sororal Publishing.

Kuh, G.D., J.H. Schuh, E.J. Whitt, and Associates. 1991. *Involving Colleges.* San Francisco: Jossey-Bass.

Kuk, L. Fall 1990. "Perspectives on Gender Differences." New Directions for Student Services No. 51.

Leatherman, C. October 27, 1993. "A Botched Search?" Chronicle of Higher Education XL(10).

Lefkowitz, M. January 19, 1994. "Combating False Theories in the Classroom." *Chronicle of Higher Education* XL(20).

Leonard, M.M., and B.A. Sigall. 1989. "Empowering Women Student Leaders: A Leadership Development Model." In *Educating the Majority: Women Challenge Tradition in Higher Education.* Pearson, Touchton, Shavlik, eds. New York: American Council on Education, Macmillan.

Leslie, L., and P. Brinkman. 1988. *The Economic Value of Higher Education.* New York: Macmillan.

Levin, J. June 1994. "Re-Conceptualizing Community College Leadership." Paper presented for the Canadian Society for the Study of Higher Education. Calgary, Alberta.

Lips, H.M. 1989. "Gender Role Socialization: Lessons in Femininity." In *Women: A Feminist Perspective.* 4th ed. J. Freeman, ed. Mountain View, Calif.: Mayfield Publishing Co.

Lussier, R.N. 1993. *Human Relations in Organizations.* Homewood, Ill.: Irwin Publishers.

MacCoby, M. 1981. *The Leader.* New York: Simon and Schuster.

MacCorquodale, P., and J. Linsink. 1991. "Integrating Women into the Curriculum: Multiple Motives and Mixed Emotions." In *Women's Higher Education in Comparative Perspective.* G.P. Kelly and S. Slaughter, eds. Netherlands: Kluwer Academic Publishers.

Masland, A.T. Winter 1985. "Organizational Culture in the Study of Higher Education." *The Review of Higher Education* 8(2): 157-68.

McClenney, B.N. 1980. *Management for Productivity.* Washington, D.C.: American Association of Community and Junior Colleges.

McQuail, D. 1983. *Mass Communication Theory: An Introduction.* Newbury Park, Calif.: Sage Publications.

Melia, J., and P. Lyttle. 1986. *Why Jenny Can't Lead: Understanding the Male Dominant System.* Grand Junction, Colo.: Operational Politics, Inc.

Miller, D., and J. Hurley. 1985. "An Experiment in Humanistic Management With Community College District Twelve, Centralia/ Olympia, Washington." Washington, D.C. ED 25 2256. 10 pp. MF-01; PC-01.

Miller, K. 1995. *Organizational Communication: Approaches and Processes*. New York: Wadsworth Publishing Co.

Miller-Solomon, B. 1985. *In the Company of Educated Women: A History of Women and Higher Education in America*. New Haven, Conn.: Yale University Press. ED 255 129.

Millett, K. 1990. *Sexual Politics: The Classic Analysis of Interplay Between Men, Women and Culture*. New York: Simon and Schuster.

Milwid, B. 1990. *Working With Men*. Hillsboro, Ore.: Beyond Words Publishing, Inc.

Minnich, E.K. 1990. *Transforming Knowledge*. Philadelphia: Temple University Press.

Mintzberg, H. 1989. *Mintzberg on Management: Inside Our Strange World of Organizations*. New York: The Free Press.

Mitchell, P.T., ed. 1993. *Cracking the Wall: Women in Higher Education Administration*. Washington, D.C.: College and University Personnel Association.

Morgan, L., and E. Clark. January 1995. "Professional Experience Profile of Female College and University Presidents: How the Glass Ceiling Was Cracked." In the proceedings of the Eighth Annual International Conference on Women in Higher Education. San Francisco.

Mott, M.C. 1997. "Women Community College Presidents' Leadership Agendas." Ph.D. dissertation, University of Arizona, Center for the Study of Higher Education.

Murray, A.J. 1986. "The Relation of Level of Education and Gender to Job Satisfaction." Ph.D. dissertation, University of Arizona.

Naisbitt, J., and P. Aburdene. 1985. *Re-inventing the Corporation*. New York: Warner Books.

Nanus, B. 1989. *The Leader's Edge: The Seven Keys to Leadership in a Turbulent World*. New York: Contemporary Books.

Nieva, V.F., and B.A. Gutek. 1980. "Sex Effects on Evaluation." *Academy of Management Review* 5: 267-76.

Northcutt, C. 1991. *Successful Career Women: Their Professional and Personal Characteristics*. New York: Greenwood Press.

O'Banion, T., ed. 1989. *Innovation in the Community College*. New York: Macmillan.

Owens, S. June 9-12, 1993. "College in Transition: A Case Study in Progress." Paper presented at the Canadian Society for the Study of Higher Education. Ottawa, Ontario.

Pearson, C.S., D.L. Shavlik, J.G. Touchton, eds. 1989. *Educating the Majority: Women Challenge Tradition in Higher Education.* New York: American Council on Education, Macmillan.

Peters, T. 1994. *Crazy Times Call for Crazy Organizations.* New York: Vintage Books.

Pfeffer, J., and A. Davis-Blake. 1987. "The Effect of the Proportion of Women on Salaries: The Case of College Administrators." *Administrative Science Quarterly* (32): 1-32.

Phillip, M.C. October 1993. "Tenure Trap: Number of Obstacles Stand in Way of Tenure for Women." *Black Issues in Higher Education* 10(17).

Refkind, L.J., and L.F. Harper. January 1995. "The Bifurcation of Individualism and Community for Women in Higher Education." In the proceedings of the Eighth Annual International Conference on Women in Higher Education. San Francisco.

Reskin, B. 1991. "Bringing the Men Back In: Sex Differentiation and the Devaluation of Women's Work." In *The Social Construction of Gender.* Newbury Park, Calif.: Sage Publications.

Reskin, B., and P. Roos, eds. 1990. *Job Queues, Gender Queues: Explaining Women's Inroads into Male Occupations.* Philadelphia: Temple University Press.

Richardson, L., and V. Taylor. 1989. *Feminist Frontiers II: Rethinking Sex, Gender, and Society.* New York: McGraw-Hill.

Rigaux, P. September 25, 1995. "Women Gain More Presidential Posts in Higher Education, ACE Report Says." *Community College Week.*

Riger, S. May 1991. "Gender Dilemmas in Sexual Harassment Policies and Procedures." *American Psychologist* 46(5): 407-505.

———. June 1992. "Epistemological Debates, Feminist Voices: Science, Social Values, and the Study of Women." *American Psychologist* 47(6): 730-40.

Ross, M., M.F. Green, C. Henderson. 1993. *The American College President: A 1993 Edition.* Washington, D.C.: American Council on Education. ED 363 171. 133 pp. MF-01; PC-06.

Roueche, J., G. Baker III, and R. Rose. 1989. *Shared Vision: Transformational Leadership in American Community Colleges.* Washington, D.C.: The Community College Press.

Samovar, L.A., and R.E. Porter. 1995. *Communication Between Cultures.* New York: Wadsworth Publishing Co.

Sandler, B., and R. Hall. 1986. "The Campus Climate Revisited: Chilly for Women Faculty, Administrators, and Graduate Students." Washington, D.C.: Project on the Status of Women,

Association of American Colleges. ED 298 837. 112 pp. MF-01; PC-05.

Scarr, S. January 1988. "Race and Gender as Psychological Variables: Social and Ethical Issues." *American Psychologist* 43(1): 15-22.

Schaef, A.W. 1985. *Women's Reality: An Emerging Female System in a White Male Society.* San Francisco: Harper and Row Publishers.

Schein, E. February 1990. "Organizational Culture." *American Psychologist* 45(2): 109-19.

Schroedel, J.R. 1985. *Alone in a Crowd.* Philadelphia: Temple University Press.

Schur, E. 1984. *Labeling Women Deviant: Gender, Stigma, and Social Control.* New York: McGraw Hill.

Schuster, M., and S. Van Dyne, eds. 1985. *Women's Place in the Academy: Transforming the Liberal Arts Curriculum.* Totowa, N.J.: Rowman and Allanheld Publishers.

Senge, P.M. 1990. *The Fifth Discipline: The Art and Practice of the Learning Organization.* New York: Doubleday/Currency Books.

Sheppard, D. 1992. "Women Managers' Perceptions of Gender and Organizational Life." In *Gendering Organizational Analysis.* Mills and Tancred, eds. London: Sage Publications.

Slaughter, S. 1993. "Retrenchment in the 1980s: The Politics and Prestige of Gender." *Journal of Higher Education* 64(3): 250-82.

Smircich, L. 1983. "Concepts of Culture and Organizational Analysis." *Administrative Science Quarterly* 28(3): 399-58. EJ 286 600.

Smith, P. 1990. *Killing the Spirit: Higher Education in America.* New York: Viking Penguin Publishers.

Steinem, G. 1994. *Moving Beyond Words.* New York: Simon and Schuster.

Tannen, D. 1990. *You Just Don't Understand: Women and Men in Conversation.* New York: Ballantine Books.

———. 1994. *Talking From 9 to 5.* New York: William Morrow.

Thompson, B.W., and S. Tyagi, eds. 1993. *Beyond a Dream Deferred: Multicultural Education and the Politics of Excellence.* Minneapolis: University of Minnesota Press.

Thorne, B. 1989. "Rethinking the Ways We Teach." In *Educating the Majority: Women Challenge Tradition in Higher Education.* Pearson, Touchton, and Shavlik, eds. New York: American Council on Education, Macmillan.

Thorne, B. 1994. *Gender Play: Girls and Boys in School.* New Brunswick, N.J.: Rutgers University Press.

Tinsley, A., C. Secor, and S. Kaplan, eds. 1984. "Women in Higher

Education Administration." New Directions for Higher Education
No. 45. San Francisco: Jossey-Bass.

Tokarczyk, M., and E. Fay, eds. 1993. *Working-Class Women in the
Academy: Laborers in the Knowledge Factory.* Amherst:
University of Massachusetts Press.

Townsend, B.K., ed. 1995. "Women Community College Faculty:
On the Margins or in the Mainstream?" In *Gender and Power in
Community Colleges.* New Directions for Community Colleges.
San Francisco: Jossey-Bass.

Trice, H.M., and J.M. Beyer 1993. *The Cultures of Work Organizations.* Englewood Cliffs, N.J.: Prentice-Hall.

University of Arizona. October 1994. "Commission on the Status of
Women: Results of Campus Climate Studies on UA Employees
and Undergraduate Students, Fall 1993-Spring 1994." Center for
Research on Undergraduate Education.

Volk, C.E. 1995. "Assessing Competing Models of Resource Al-
location at a Public Research 1 University Through Multivariate
Analysis of State Funding." Ph.D. dissertation, University of
Arizona.

Wabnik, A. September 18, 1995. "Female Profs Earn Far Less Than
UA Men." *Arizona Daily Star.*

Wall, B., R.S. Solum, and M.R. Sobol. 1992. *The Visionary Leader.*
Rocklin, Calif.: Prima Publishing.

Warner, R., and L. DeFleur. 1993. "Career Paths of Women in
Higher Education Administration." In *Cracking the Wall.* Mitchell, ed. Washington, D.C.: College and University Personnel Association.

Washington, V., and W. Harvey. 1989. *Affirmative Rhetoric, Neg-
ative Action: African-American and Hispanic Faculty in
Predominantly White Institutions.* ASHE-ERIC Higher Education
Report No. 2. Washington, D.C.: The George Washington
University, Graduate School of Education and Human
Development. ED 316 075. 128 pp. MF-01; PC-06.

Wenninger, Mary Dee, ed., *Women in Higher Education.* 1995.
Volume 4, (N1-12). Madison, WI: Women in Higher Education.
ED 392 319. 204 pp. MF-01; PC-09.

West, C., and D. Zimmerman. 1991. "Doing Gender." In *The Social
Construction of Gender.* Newbury Park, Calif.: Sage Publications.

Wilcox, J.R., and S.L. Ebbs. 1992. *The Leadership Compass: Values
and Ethics in Higher Education.* ASHE-ERIC Higher Education
Report No. 1. Washington, D.C.: The George Washington
University, Graduate School of Education and Human
Development. ED 347 955. 129 pp. MF-01; PC-06.

Wilkerson, M.B. 1989. "Majority, Minority and the Numbers Game." In *Educating the Majority: Women Challenge Tradition in Higher Education*. New York: American Council on Education, Macmillan.

Wilson, R. November 24, 1995. "Equal Pay, Equal Work? Male Professors Claim Salary Equity Studies Discriminate Against Them." *Chronicle of Higher Education.*

———. April 4, 1997. "A College Debates Whether New Accreditor Promotes Rigor or Curbs Intellectual Diversity." *Chronicle of Higher Education.*

Wilson, R.E. June 1995. "Female Leadership Issues in Higher Education." Presentation at Women's Leadership Conference. Wells College, Aurora, N.Y.

INDEX

A

AACJC. See American Association of Community and Junior Colleges

AALE. See American Academy of Liberal Education

academic change strategies, 80–85

academic posts only accesible to single women, 10

Acker (1991) gender-neutral job
  has no sex or emotion or procreation ability, 60

Adams (1995)
  measured sex-role orientation and career satisfaction, 51

administrative leadership associated with an image of
  a rational, logical, objective and aggressive male, 14

affirmative action
  as a cause for perpetuation of the gender gap, 14–18
  Hanna (1988) study of, 16
    importance of, 83–84
    only nonwhite women had overwhelming support for, 16
    party affiliation as greatest predictor of opinion regarding, 16
    programs caught in a morass of opposition and
      uncertainty, 17

African-Americans
  "concrete wall" as term for artificial barriers to advance of, 17

American Academy of Liberal Education, 20

The American College President: A 1993 Edition, 6, 31

American Council on Education-Office of Women in Higher
  Education, 6

Amey and Twombly (1992) found "great man"
  to be a prevalent feature in community college literature, 77

analysis of institutional leadership styles
  based on perceptions of faculty regarding their chief executive
    officer, 56

androgynous individuals
  tend to be more flexiable and have healthier self-esteem, 51

The Androgynous Manager, 53

androgyny as means of attaining higher education positions, 77

Apollo College, ix

Astin and Davis (1985)
  married women's careers resembled those of men more
    closely than did the professional careers of single
    women, 24

attribution theory can give insight into issues related to tenure
  procedures, 24

authoritarian leadership styles

come from false assumptions about human nature, 64–65
authority
    formal right to get people to do things or control resources, 43
autocratic leaders, 55

B

Baldridge et al. (1977) description of three frames of reference, 61
Baylor University, 20
behavior such as aggressiveness, competitiveness and dominance
    receive different reactions depending upon sex of the actor, 74
Bell (1997) affirmative-action programs
        caught in a morass of opposition and uncertainty, 17
Bellas (1993)
        analysis of wage data from Carnegie Foundation survey,
          35–36
"benevolent patriarch," 82
Bennis (1991)
    challenged dominant norms with questions about traditional
        assumptions, 21
    four leadership competencies that draw people to a leader, 66
    four themes evident if leadership is effective in empowering the
        workforce, 64
    many institutions very well managed and poorly led, 55
Bergquist (1992) explored and evaluated Bolman and Deal's
        and Bimbaum's frames as applied to collegiate
        institutions, 61
Birnbaum (1988)
    most presidents of higher education institutions would have to be
        satisfied with role as a coordinator of a complex institution, 66
    reevaluated Bolman and Deal's four frames based on higher
        education organizations, 61
Blackmore and Kewway (1993)
    provide feminist introduction for contemplating educational
        administration in a societal context, 58
Bloom (1987) *The Closing of the American Mind*
    femininism as the latest enemy of the vitality of the classic
        text, 19
"blue chip" community, 77
Bolman and deal (1984) Four Frames of Reference, 61
Bond, Sheryl
        studied leadership experiences and perceptions of
          Canadian university leaders, 49
"bossy," 50

Bryman (1992)
>   managers tends to be more practical and decisive while
>   leaders more visionary and flexible, 82
>   participative leadership enhances job satisfaction, 61

Bryn Mawr college founded in 1885, 10

Bureaucratic/Structural Frame, 61–62
>   leadership literature reveals a strong leaning in higher
>   education institutions for, 68

Bush administration carried forward Reagan administration rhetoric
>   regarding male privilege in a family model, 15

C

California State University System
>   abolishment of affirmative action at, 17

Canadian university leaders
>   team of researchers studied leadership experiences and
>   perceptions of, 49

career mobility necessary for female advancement, 81

Career Satisfaction, 51–52

"caretaker"
>   woman's role as, 58

care/connection voice, 67
>   "prefer collaborative discussion and learning by listening," 45
>   response mode for women, 45
>   women have a preference for, 67

Carnegie Foundation 1984 survey of women wages, 35–36

"catalyst," leader as, 62

Center for Values and Research in Dallas, 74

charisma, 65

children as a threat to tenure, 32–33

"chilly climate," 28

Chliwniak, Luba
>   background of, ix
>   study of leadership-evaluation criteria, 85

Chodorow on social orientation
>   men's is positional while women's is personal, 45

The Closing of the American Mind, Bloom (1987), 19

cognitive development theory, 67

collegial approach
>   may have horizontal leadership or may have several power
>   centers, 65

Collegium/Human Resource Frame, 62

communication patterns, 49–51

community colleges listed with the AACJC in 1990 study
 less than 10 percent were found to have academic deans
  with women's first names, 40
comparable-worth salary plan downside, 38
compatibility cycle need to break, ix
"concrete wall"
 term for artificial barriers to advance of African-Americans, 17
constructivism, 19
conversational rituals common among women, 50
"cootie game," 75
Cornell University gave equal status to women and men in 1872, 10
Covey (1991)
 challenged dominant norms with questions about traditional
  assumptions, 21
 six conditions of empowerment, 65
coworkers are more negative toward women managers then to
 male managers who lack human-relations skills, 74
Cracking the Wall, 77
critical mass for granting of women faculty tenure, 12, 23
critical theorist role
 explore and uncover imbalances in power and make them
  known to oppressed groups, 15
cultural norming
 certain ideas excluded through, 78
culture, 59
 key components of a strong, 13
 personifies the institution's understood goals, 63
current data on women in higher education, 6
current leadership theorists model
 encompasses strong human-relations skills, a humanistic
  approach, collegiality and consensus building, 69
curriculum and scholarship
 as a cause for perpetuation of the gender gap, 18–22
Cybernetic System, 62–63

D
Desjardins (1989)
 discusses the meaning of Gilligan's "different voice"
  through cognitive development, 60
 example of feminized leadership scholar, 21
 utilizes Gilligan's (1982) coding system to analyze if gender
  determines leadership modes for community colleges
  CEOs, 67

"different voice"

discussion of the meaning of, 60

disciplines with many women faculty retrenched at higher rates

than in more highly male-dominated disciplines, 23

discourse analysis

as a means of deciphering historical and current

perspectives on college leadership, 77

disparity between numbers of women leaders in relationship to the

numbers of women who earn advanced degrees, 5

"doublespeak" internally and externally regarding leaders, 85

Drucker, Peter, 2

Drucker (1967)

an organization which just perpetuates today's level has lost

the capacity to adapt, 64

four basic requirements for effective CEO human

relations, 66

knowledge worker cannot be supervised closely or in

detail, 61

model encompasses strong human-relations skills, a

humanistic approach, collegiality and consensus

building, 69

E

Eagly and Johnson (1990)

meta-analysis of gender and leadership style, 46

Eagly and Karau (1991)

in orginally leaderless groups, men emerged as leaders to a

greater extent than did women, 46

Eagly, Makhijani, and Klonsky (1992), 73

traditional masculine leadership styles seen as more

favorable for male leaders, 73

women should avoid roles and situations in which men

serve as evaluators, 23

education as a vehicle for making women better wives, homemak-

ers and mothers, 9

effective human relations by a CEO

four basic requirements for, 66

emerging (response mode) perceptions of leadership

women more than men appear to exhibit, 49

emerging leadership mode views

organization as a circle, 64

England (1992) provides guidance

for determining occupationally segregated workforce, 83

Epstein (1988)
> gender diferences are not empirically real, 49

equality cannot be externally assigned until it has been internally perceived, 85

evaluations of occupational prestige as a cause for perpetuation of the gender gap, 39

F

"facilitator"
> leader as, 62

faculty and tenure as cause for perpetuation of gender gap, 22–25

federal monitoring offices
> effects of downsizing on affirmative action, 15

"feeling" category for decision making, 45

female. See also women
> attempt to adopt male behavior to fit into male-dominated positions somewhat less than successful, 6

> "glass ceiling" as term for artificial barriers to advance of, 17

> interviewees equaled power with giving and care, 43

> leadership perceived as more task-oriented than male leaders, 73

> system power is considered limitless, 43

femininism
> as the latest enemy of the vitality of the classic text, 19

feminist introduction for contemplating educational administration in a societal context, 58

feminist postmodernism, 26

feminist scholarship
> as a system of values that challenges male dominance, 26

> as a risky career decision, 27–28

> aversion to has left members of the academy uninformed as well as misinformed, 78

feminized leadership scholars, 21

feminizing of leadership roles
> would lead to lowered prestige and economic value of the position, 39

Ferguson (1984) "a nonbureaucratic collective life," 58

fifth discipline, 2

Finkel and Olswang (1995)
> study of assistant female professors at large public university, 32

first universities to accept women, 10

Flynn (1993) women not selected for leadership roles
> because of belief that men prefer to work with other men, 4

Four Frames of Reference, 61

four leadership competencies that draw people to a leader, 66

future of women in higher education leadership

    insight into the, 8

future research suggested direction, 84–85

G

Gallimore-McKee (1991)

    analysis of institutional leadership styles based on percep-
    tions of faculty regarding their chief executive officer, 56

"Garbage cans"

    provide outlets for unrelated and unresolved problems for
    institutional members, 62

Garfield (1992), 2

gender

  relevance in leadership conceptualizations, 59–61

    and ethnicity negatively affect amount of resources allo-
    cated to the department, 37

    "and the Emergence of Leaders," 46

    as achieved status constructed through psychological, cul-
    tural, and social means, 59

gender differences

    are not empirically real, 49

    in behavioral styles which then result in differences in
    evaluations, 74

    theory of Gilligan (1989, 1982), 44–45

gender gap

  eight persistence factors in the perpetuation of, 14–39

    more related to inequity than to difference, 53

gender-neutral job has no sex or emotion or procreation ability, 60

gender-related

    characteristics described as innate to most women
    encompass characteristics claimed to be most effective, 2

    communication patterns constrain how girls and women
    express leadership, 50

gender-role theory, 73

"generic man," 13

Gilligan (1982)

    coding system used to analyze if gender determines leader-
    ship modes for community colleges CEOs, 67

    female interviewees equated power with giving and care, 43

    men fear becoming entrapped in webs of interconnection, 60

    moral reasoning research of, 67

research on women's moral development of, 21

Gilligan (1989, 1982)

       theory on gender differences of, 44–45

Gilligan/Kohlberg ethical-dilemma research comparisons of moral
       development in males and females, 44

Glass Ceiling, 52–54

       as term for artificial barriers to advance of females, 17

       result of a woman being unlike her predecessor, 4

"go-getters," 50

"great books" curriculum of Thomas Acquinas College, 20

great person theory of leadership

    still prevalent in higher education scholarship and practice, 77

"guardian" role of leader, 62

Gutek (1989) coined the term "sex-role spillover," 52

H

Hall, Roberta, 28

Hanna (1988) study of previously conducted studies in the area of
       affirmative action, 16

Harding (in Riger 1992) challenges neutrality of science, 26

Harvard College

    first institution of higher education in the United States, 9

Helgesen (1990)

       challenged dominant norms with questions about
          traditional assumptions, 21

       chronicled leadership styles of four women chief executive
          officers, 44

Helgesen (1995 & 1990) example of feminized leadership
       scholar, 21

Hensel (1991)

       time line for equal representation in all areas of academe, 22

hidden curriculum behaviors and gestures, 29–30

"hierarchy of difference" based on economic need, 15

higher education

       be better if reflected the values of women leaders?, 4

       reserved for men rationale, 9

high task/high relationship style

       most prevalent among presidents, 56

I

impact of sex on administrative style and success, 74

implications of emerging posthierarchical feminized leadership
       style in academe, 79–80

incremental changes can be extremely effective, 81
Individual Characteristics, 65–68
informal network system
    women for the most part have been excluded from, 40–41
institutional culture, 63
institutions can be very well managed and poorly led, 55
institutions of higher reputational ranking
    have even less women in upper level positions, ix
"interior colonization," 13, 60
internal cultural tasks, 59

J

James Madison College, 20
job satisfaction for women in higher education dependent upon
        motivators such as job level, tenure and department, 51
Johnsrud and Heck (1994), 37
justice voice
    men have a preference for, 67
        response mode for women, 45

K

Kandiyoti (1991)
    baselines from which women negotiate and strategize through
        "patriarchal bargains," 52
Kandyoti (1989)
        chronicles how women "bargain with the patriarchy," 32
Kanter (1977), 4
        not male and female characteristics that create gender
            differences but structure of the organization, 59
Kelly (1991)
        impact of sex on administrative style and success, 74
        utilizes segmented labor-market theory to analyze overall
            gendered picture of U.S. economy, 57
Kent State University gender based differences in salary, 36
Kohlberg's six-stage theory challenged by Gilligan
        as being inappropriate for women's development, 45

L

The Leader, 56
leaders
        as heterosexual, white, competitive, rational and male, 58
        concerned with management of people, 1
        people who do the right thing, 55

values and goals reflected in functioning of the institution?, 4

leadership, 55-56

concept of effective, 55

current theorists model emphasize strong human-
relations, 1–2

deals with the top line, 79

effective in empowering workforce then four themes
evident, 64

equated to power, 43

list of needed skills, 66

learning organizations focus on development of decentralized,
nonhierarchical and employee dedicated, 69

"legend" of the institution, 63

Leonard and Sigall (1989)

women must become more effective power users or academy
will remain male-dominant system, 43

Lesh-Laurie, Georgia

interview with, 83

Levin, John, xi

low task/high relationship style most prefered among faculty, 56

M

MacCoby (1981) provides perspective of
society's expectations and acceptance of leaders, 56

*Making Sense of Administrative Leadership: The "L" Word in Higher
Education*, 61

male filters rendered women's experiences as invisible, 52

male models of career advancement

as greatest inhibitor to women's success, 57

males as leaders

presumed assumption of natural affinity of, 3

management focuses on the bottom line, 79

managers as people who do things right, 55

married women's careers resembled those of men more closely
than did the professional careers of single women, 24

Marx

critical approaches to understanding organiztional culture
have philosophical roots in the work of, 15

masculine skills

women aspiring to administrative positions should
cultivate, 51

Masland (1985)

institutional culture establishes a set of expectations and norms through purpose, commitment and order, 63

Men and Women of the Corporation, 59

men. *See also* male *and* males

disproportionately represented at upper leadership levels, ix

fear becoming entrapped in webs of interconnection, 60

have stake in maintaining differentiation of spheres, 4

respond to women's intrusion in the workforce by
emphasizing how men and women differ, 52

men's communication pattern

to negotiate status and often engage in verbal competition,
49–50

meta-analysis in of gender and the evaluation of leaders, 731992

"micro-inequities," 28

need to eliminate, 82

micro-narratives as opposed to universals and essentials in
knowledge, 22

Miller and Hurley (1985)

only followers con confer leadership, 77

Millett (1990), 13

"interior colonization," 60

Milwid (1990), 4

professional women viewed power not as a right of position but
as a commodity which grew with sharing, 43–44

strongest evidence of sex difference in leadership style, 46

Women experience organizational life with deep ambivalence
due to conflicting values and modes, 46

Milwid (1992)

women managers attempted not to challenge the prevailing sex
norms in study of, 74

Mintzberg (1989)

list of needed leadership skills, 66

results as a standard for comparing women leaders, 44

Mitchell (1993)

androgyny as means of attaining higher education administrative
positions, 77

moral reasoning research of Carol Gilligan, 67

Morgan and Clark (1995), 8

Morill Land Grant Act effect, 10

Mott, Maxine, xi

Mott (1997)

research on if female community college presidents incorporate a
feminist perspective in their institutional agendas, 85

Mount Holyoke college founded in 1888, 10

Munk, Linda, xi
Murray (1986)
>job satisfaction for women in higher education dependent upon motivators such as job level, tenure and department, 51
Myers and Briggs typographical profile
>somewhat confirms Gilligan's observed differences, 45

N

Naisbitt and Aburdene (1985)
>many of the new models for reinventing organizations stem from the impact of women in the workforce, 53
Nanus (1989)
>challenged dominant norms with questions about traditional assumptions, 21
>qualities of effective leadership lacking in America today, 57
National Association of Scholars, 20
"natural" gender roles for women
>rationale for emphasis on, 52
"Negative feedback loops" created and reinforced
>to continually assess institutional performance, 63
"nonbureaucratic collective life," 58–59
Normative Leadership Theory, 55–56
Northcutt (1991)
>women define career success without power orientation, 43
Northern Arizona University gender based differences in salary, 36
nurturers
>effect in society of women as, 30

O

occupationally segregated workforce
>guidance for determining, 83
Organizational Contexts, 61–65
organization as a circle
>emerging leadership mode, 64
organization as a pyramid
>traditional views of higher education leadership, 64
Organized Anarchy/Symbolic Frame
>leader as "facilitator," 62
Owens (1993) case study on a college in leadership transition, 85

P

participative

leaders, 55
    leadership enhances job satisfaction, 61
    style less prevalent among men, 73
participatory leadership
  more related to women's leadership style then to men's, 70
"patriarchal bargains," 52
patriarchal systems tactics that are negative for women, 73–74
Patton (1990) women managers in higher education
    less interested in power and control, 43
pedagogy as a cause for perpetuation of the gender gap, 28–30
percentage of academics that are women, 3
personal, family, and career issues as a cause for perpetuation of
  the gender gap, 30–33
Peters (1994), 2
  advocates replacing bureaucracies wih fluid, interdependent
    groups of problem solvers, 69
  challenged dominant norms with questions about traditional
    assumptions, 21
    encourages model with strong human-relations skills, a
      humanistic aproach, collegiality and consensus
      building, 69
Pfeffer and Davis-Blake (1987), 39
  "women's work" description as less valuable and should cost
    less than work by men, 37
Pima Community College, ix
Political Frame, 62
polls on affirmative-action, 16
positivism asks what are the answers, 19
posthierarchical model for organizations, 2
postmodern theorists arguing that living in a different world, 22
Power
  ability to influence decisions and control resources, 43
  gender differences in definition of, 43
prejudices toward employment & advancement of married women,
    11
presidents of higher education institutions
    position has a high impact upon the institution, 67
    role of, 66
Professional Experience Profile, 8
professional women
    viewed power not as a right of position but as a commodity
    which grew with sharing, 43–44
proportion of women in an occupation

negatively related to the prestige of the occupation, 38

Q
qualities of effective leadership lacking in America today, 57

R
Reagan administration rhetoric regarding male privilege in a family
       model carried forward by Bush administration, 15
regression analyses of resource allocation in higher education, 37
research on women's moral development by Gilligan (1982), 21
Reskin (1991) on how men respond to women's intrusion in the
       workforce by emphasizing how men and women differ, 52
Reskin and Roos (1990)
   men have stake in maintaining differentiation of spheres, 4
reverse discrimination
   affirmative action as reason for, 17
Rhodes College, 20
       institution in which faculty members opposed the AALE
         accreditation process and standards, 20
Rigaux (1995), 6
role theory and social construction of gender categories, 59
Ross, Green, and Henderson (1993) provide insight into
       the future of women in higher education leadership, 8
Roueche, Baker, and Rose (1989)
       described "blue chip" community, 77

S
Sandler, Bernice, 28
Sargent (1981) men and women should learn from another
       without abandoning successful traits they already possess, 53
Schaef (1985)
   men's concept of power is based on a scarcity model, 43
       describes tactics utilized in patriarchal systems that are
         negative for women, 73–74
Schein (1990)
   internal cultural tasks of, 59
segmented labor-market theory, 57
Seidman (1985) study of community college faculty
       women express concern on effect of sexist attitudes in, 31
Senge (1990), 2
       focuses on development of decentralized, nonhierarchical
        and employee dedicated learning organizations, 69
       structures of which we are unaware hold us prisoner, 71

systematic structures are concerned with key
interrelationship that influence behavior over time, 79
sex-role orientation and career satisfaction, 51
"sex-role spillover," 52
sexual harassment
as a cause for perpetuation of the gender gap, 33–35
viewed as a low risk behavior, 34
Sheppard (1992)
male filters rendered women's experiences as invisible, 52
women managers attempted not to challenge the prevailing
sex norms in study of, 74
women experience organizational life with deep
ambivalence due to conflicting values and modes, 46
situational leadership, 56
six conditions of empowerment, 65
Slaughter, Sheila, xi
Slaughter (1993) research on retrenchment in the 1980's, 23
small sample size causes lack of focus on race, ethnicity, and/or
social class, 2–3
Smith college, founded in 1871, 10
social constructionists
argue that characteristics of the care/connection (response)
mode are the result of societal expectations, 68
social exchange theory, 66
societal conceptualizations, 56–59
sociolinguistic patterns of men and women in relationships and at
work, 50
sources of power are positional and personal, 44
Steinem (1994)
androgynous individuals tend to be more flexiable and
have healthier self-esteem, 51
Bush administration carried forward Reagan administration
rhetoric regarding male privilege in a family model, 15
vision of the world not seen through the eyes of only males
would add depth and new perspectives, 52–53
"stoppers" for "deviant" behavior, 73–74
strategies for academic change, 80–85
structure of the organization not the characteristics
of men and women that create gender differences, 59
structures of which we are unaware hold us prisoner, 71
studies of sociolinguistic patterns of men and women in
relationships and at work, 50
study of assistant female professors at large public university

by Finkel and Olswang (1995), 32
"superachiever" as only female considered as equal to a male, 31
symbolic frame
    strong support in literature for higher education institutions, 68
symbolic organization ultimately hierarchical
        but has appearance of being collaborative, 65
systematic structures are concerned with key interrelationship
        that influence behavior over time, 79

T

Tannen (1990, 1994) studies of sociolinguistic patterns
            of men and women in relationships and at work, 50
tenure strong predictor for positions as chief academic officers, 25
Texas abolishment of affirmative action in, 17
"thinking" category for decision making, 45
Thomas Acquinas College
    "great books" curriculum of, 20
Thorne (1994) gender-related communication patterns
            constrain how girls and women express leadership, 50
time line for equal representation in all areas of academe, 22
Title VII of the U.S. Civil Rights Act
        sexual harassment as a violation of, 33
Townsend (1995)
            two-year institutions may have less-sexist environments
                because tenure process usually based on length of
                service, 23
Traditional and Emerging Leadership Values and Modes, 47–48
trait theory, 65, 68
transformational leadership, 56
    becoming synonymous with cultural management of higher
            education institutions, 63
            needs to be promoted and developed by women, 81–82
two-year institutions may have less-sexist environments
            because tenure process usually based on length of
                service, 23
types of people that are liked, ix

U

University of Arizona gender based differences in salary, 36
University of California at Davis gender based salary differences, 36
University of Colorado at Denver, 83
University of Dallas accredited by AALE, 20
University of Manitoba, 49

university or college presidents in 1990 "snapshot", 6
U.S. Bureau of Labor statistics on female professor earnings, 36

V

Vassar college founded in 1865, 10
Virginia Commonwealth University, 36
    gender based differences in salary at, 36
vision amplified through institutional behavior, 63
visionary, participative leadership concept, 60–61
Volk (1995)
  regression analyses of resource allocation in higher
    education, 37
Vroom and Yetton's Normative Leadership Theory, 55–56

W

wage gap as a cause for perpetuation of the gender gap, 35–38
web of inclusion, 2
  as new posthierarchical model for organization, 69
Wellesly college founded in 1870, 10
white male group as standard for good behavior then behavior of
    women and ethnic minorities is likely to seem
      negative, 20–21
White Male System power conceived in a zero-sum fashion, 43
Wilcox and Ebbs (1992)
    president's position has a high impact upon the
     institution, 67
Wilson, Gov. Pete
    campaign to abolish affirmative-action policies, 17
women. *See also* female
women adopted male standards of success, 5
women and men leaders appear to be more alike than different
    when position is the primary studied variable, 49
women underrepresented in all leadership ranks in academe, 1
women "bargain with the patriarchy," 32
women define career success without power orientation, 43
women experience organizational life
    with deep ambivalence due to conflicting values and
     modes, 46
women express concern on effect of sexist attitudes in
    Seidman (1985) study of community college faculty, 31
women leaders
    adopt behaviors or appear to behave in a fashion similar to
     their male colleagues, 46

evaluation, 73–74
negatively evaluated when exhibiting masculine leadership
styles, 74
not supported when fill role in assertative manner, 50
time required for tangible results as rationale for lack of, 69
women managers
attempted not to challenge the prevailing sex norms, 74
in higher education less interested in power and control, 43
women more than men appear to exhibit
emerging (response mode) perceptions of leadership, 49
women receive lower salaries than men, ix
women's cognitive development has a possible negative effect, 84
women's communication pattern
generally used to elicit cooperation or create rapport, 49
women's filling of position lowers occupational prestige, 39
women should avoid roles and situations in which men serve as
evaluators, 23
women's Leadership and the Leadership Frames, 68–70
women's leadership styles, 44–46, 49
would it change way higher education conceived and organized?, 4
women's salaries in academe negative effect, 36
women's studies
and feminist scholarship as cause for perpetuation of
gender gap, 25–28
marginalized location renders problematic for faculty, 27
perceived as a place where "women libbers" espouse theories
that were contrary to inclusion in so-called normal
curriculum, 26
"women's work" as institutionalized concept including idea that
less valuable and should cost less than work by men, 37
working in centers rather than having a home department
impedes tenure, salary, and promotion decisions, 25

ASHE-ERIC HIGHER EDUCATION REPORTS

Since 1983, the Association for the Study of Higher Education (ASHE) and the Educational Resources Information Center (ERIC) Clearinghouse on Higher Education, a sponsored project of the Graduate School of Education and Human Development at The George Washington University, have cosponsored the ASHE-ERIC Higher Education Report series. This volume is the twenty-fifth overall and the eighth to be published by the Graduate School of Education and Human Development at The George Washington University.

Each monograph is the definitive analysis of a tough higher education problem, based on thorough research of pertinent literature and institutional experiences. Topics are identified by a national survey. Noted practitioners and scholars are then commissioned to write the reports, with experts providing critical reviews of each manuscript before publication.

Eight monographs (10 before 1985) in the ASHE-ERIC Higher Education Report series are published each year and are available on individual and subscription bases. To order, use the order form on the last page of this book.

Qualified persons interested in writing a monograph for the ASHE-ERIC Higher Education Report series are invited to submit a proposal to the National Advisory Board. As the preeminent literature review and issue analysis series in higher education, the Higher Education Reports are guaranteed wide dissemination and national exposure for accepted candidates. Execution of a monograph requires at least a minimal familiarity with the ERIC database, including *Resources in Education* and the current *Index to Journals in Education*. The objective of these reports is to bridge conventional wisdom with practical research. Prospective authors are strongly encouraged to call Dr. Fife at 800-773-3742.

For further information, write to
    ASHE-ERIC Higher Education Reports
    The George Washington University
    One Dupont Circle, Suite 630
    Washington, DC 20036
Or phone (202) 296-2597; toll free: 800-773-ERIC.

Write or call for a complete catalog.

Visit our Web site at http://www.gwu.edu/~eriche

ADVISORY BOARD

James Earl Davis
University of Delaware at Newark

Cassie Freeman
Peabody College–Vanderbilt University

Susan Frost
Emory University

Mildred Garcia
Arizona State University West

James Hearn
University of Georgia

Philo Hutcheson
Georgia State University

CONSULTING EDITORS

Thomas A. Angelo
AAHE Assessment Forum

Sandra Beyer
University of Texas at El Paso

Robert Boice
State University of New York–Stony Brook

Steve Brigham
American Association for Higher Education

Ivy E. Broder
The American University

Robert A. Cornesky
Cornesky and Associates, Inc.

Barbara Gross Davis
University of California at Berkeley

James R. Davis
Center for Academic Quality and Assessment of Student
  Learning

Cheryl Falk
Yakima Valley Community College

L. Dee Fink
University of Oklahoma

Anne H. Frank
American Association of University Professors

Joseph E. Gilmore
Northwest Missouri State University

Dean L. Hubbard
Northwest Missouri State University

Mardee Jenrette
Miami-Dade Community College

Clara M. Lovett
Northern Arizona University

Laurence R. Marcus
Rowan College

Robert Menges
Northwestern University

Diane E. Morrison
Centre for Curriculum and Professional Development

L. Jackson Newell
University of Utah

Steven G. Olswang
University of Washington

Brent Ruben
State University of New Jersey–Rutgers

Sherry Sayles-Folks
Eastern Michigan University

Daniel Seymour
Claremont College–California

Pamela D. Sherer
The Center for Teaching Excellence

Marilla D. Svinicki
University of Texas–Austin

David Sweet
OERI, U.S. Department of Education

Gershon Vincow
Syracuse University

W. Allan Wright
Dalhousie University

Donald H. Wulff
University of Washington

Manta Yorke
Liverpool John Moores University

REVIEW PANEL

Charles Adams
University of Massachusetts–Amherst

Louis Albert
American Association for Higher Education

Richard Alfred
University of Michigan

Henry Lee Allen
University of Rochester

Philip G. Altbach
Boston College

Marilyn J. Amey
University of Kansas

Kristine L. Anderson
Florida Atlantic University

Karen D. Arnold
Boston College

Robert J. Barak
Iowa State Board of Regents

Alan Bayer
Virginia Polytechnic Institute and State University

John P. Bean
Indiana University–Bloomington

John M. Braxton
Peabody College, Vanderbilt University

Ellen M. Brier
Tennessee State University

Barbara E. Brittingham
The University of Rhode Island

Dennis Brown
University of Kansas

Peter McE. Buchanan
Council for Advancement and Support of Education

Patricia Carter
University of Michigan

John A. Centra
Syracuse University

Arthur W. Chickering
George Mason University

Darrel A. Clowes
Virginia Polytechnic Institute and State University

Cynthia S. Dickens
Mississippi State University

Deborah M. DiCroce
Piedmont Virginia Community College

Sarah M. Dinham
University of Arizona

Kenneth A. Feldman
State University of New York–Stony Brook

Dorothy E. Finnegan
The College of William & Mary

Mildred Garcia
Montclair State College

Rodolfo Z. Garcia
Commission on Institutions of Higher Education

Kenneth C. Green
University of Southern California

James Hearn
University of Georgia

Edward R. Hines
Illinois State University

Deborah Hunter
University of Vermont

Philo Hutcheson
Georgia State University

Bruce Anthony Jones
University of Pittsburgh

Elizabeth A. Jones
The Pennsylvania State University

Kathryn Kretschmer
University of Kansas

Marsha V. Krotseng
State College and University Systems of West Virginia

George D. Kuh
Indiana University–Bloomington

Daniel T. Layzell
University of Wisconsin System

Patrick G. Love
Kent State University

Cheryl D. Lovell
State Higher Education Executive Officers

Meredith Jane Ludwig
American Association of State Colleges and Universities

Dewayne Matthews
Western Interstate Commission for Higher Education

Mantha V. Mehallis
Florida Atlantic University

Toby Milton
Essex Community College

James R. Mingle
State Higher Education Executive Officers

John A. Muffo
Virginia Polytechnic Institute and State University

L. Jackson Newell
Deep Springs College

James C. Palmer
Illinois State University

Robert A. Rhoads
The Pennsylvania State University

G. Jeremiah Ryan
Harford Community College

Mary Ann Danowitz Sagaria
The Ohio State University

Daryl G. Smith
The Claremont Graduate School

William G. Tierney
University of Southern California

Susan B. Twombly
University of Kansas

Robert A. Walhaus
University of Illinois–Chicago

Harold Wechsler
University of Rochester

Elizabeth J. Whitt
University of Illinois–Chicago

Michael J. Worth
The George Washington University

RECENT TITLES

Volume 25 ASHE-ERIC Higher Education Reports

1. A Culture for Academic Excellence: Implementing the Quality
   Principles in Higher Education
   Jann E. Freed, Marie R. Klugman, and Jonathan D. Fife

2. From Discipline to Development: Rethinking Student
   Conduct in Higher Education
   Michael Dannells

3. Academic Controversy: Enriching College Instruction
   Through Intellectual Conflict
   David W. Johnson, Roger T. Johnson, and Karl A. Smith

Volume 24 ASHE-ERIC Higher Education Reports

1. Tenure, Promotion, and Reappointment: Legal and
   Administrative Implications (951)
   Benjamin Baez and John A. Centra

2. Taking Teaching Seriously: Meeting the Challenge of
   Instructional Improvement (952)
   Michael B. Paulsen and Kenneth A. Feldman

3. Empowering the Faculty: Mentoring Redirected and Renewed
   (953)
   Gaye Luna and Deborah L. Cullen

4. Enhancing Student Learning: Intellectual, Social, and
   Emotional Integration (954)
   Anne Goodsell Love and Patrick G. Love

5. Benchmarking in Higher Education: Adapting Best Practices
   to Improve Quality (955)
   Jeffrey W. Alstete

6. Models for Improving College Teaching: A Faculty Resource
   (956)
   Jon E. Travis

7. Experiential Learning in Higher Education: Linking Classroom
   and Community (957)
   Jeffrey A. Cantor

8. Successful Faculty Development and Evaluation: The Complete Teaching Portfolio (958)
   John P. Murray

Volume 23 ASHE-ERIC Higher Education Reports

1. The Advisory Committee Advantage: Creating an Effective
   Strategy for Programmatic Improvement (941)
   Lee Teitel

2. Collaborative Peer Review: The Role of Faculty in Improving
   College Teaching (942)
   Larry Keig and Michael D. Waggoner

3. Prices, Productivity, and Investment: Assessing Financial Strategies in Higher Education (943)
   Edward P. St. John

4. The Development Officer in Higher Education: Toward an Understanding of the Role (944)
   Michael J. Worth and James W. Asp II

5. Measuring Up: The Promises and Pitfalls of Performance Indicators in Higher Education (945)
   Gerald Gaither, Brian P. Nedwek, and John E. Neal

6. A New Alliance: Continuous Quality and Classroom Effectiveness (946)
   Mimi Wolverton

7. Redesigning Higher Education: Producing Dramatic Gains in Student Learning (947)
   Lion F. Gardiner

8. Student Learning outside the Classroom: Transcending Artificial Boundaries (948)
   George D. Kuh, Katie Branch Douglas, Jon P. Lund, and Jackie Ramin-Gyurnek

Volume 22 ASHE-ERIC Higher Education Reports

1. The Department Chair: New Roles, Responsibilities, and Challenges (931)
   Alan T. Seagren, John W. Creswell, and Daniel W. Wheeler

2. Sexual Harassment in Higher Education: From Conflict to Community (932)
   Robert O. Riggs, Patricia H. Murrell, and JoAnne C. Cutting

3. Chicanos in Higher Education: Issues and Dilemmas for the 21st Century (933)
   Adalberto Aguirre Jr., and Ruben O. Martinez

4. Academic Freedom in American Higher Education: Rights, Responsibilities, and Limitations (934)
   Robert K. Poch

5. Making Sense of the Dollars: The Costs and Uses of Faculty Compensation (935)
   Kathryn M. Moore and Marilyn J. Amey

6. Enhancing Promotion, Tenure, and Beyond: Faculty Socialization as a Cultural Process (936)
   William G. Tierney and Robert A. Rhoads

7. New Perspectives for Student Affairs Professionals: Evolving Realities, Responsibilities, and Roles (937)
   Peter H. Garland and Thomas W. Grace

8. Turning Teaching into Learning: The Role of Student Responsibility in the Collegiate Experience (938)
   Todd M. Davis and Patricia Hillman Murrell

Volume 21 ASHE-ERIC Higher Education Reports

1. The Leadership Compass: Values and Ethics in Higher Education (921)
   John R. Wilcox and Susan L. Ebbs

2. Preparing for a Global Community: Achieving an International Perspective in Higher Education (922)
   Sarah M. Pickert

3. Quality: Transforming Postsecondary Education (923)
   Ellen Earle Chaffee and Lawrence A. Sherr

4. Faculty Job Satisfaction: Women and Minorities in Peril (924)
   Martha Wingard Tack and Carol Logan Patitu

5. Reconciling Rights and Responsibilities of Colleges and Students: Offensive Speech, Assembly, Drug Testing, and Safety (925)
   Annette Gibbs

6. Creating Distinctiveness: Lessons from Uncommon Colleges and Universities (926)
   Barbara K. Townsend, L. Jackson Newell, and Michael D. Wiese

7. Instituting Enduring Innovations: Achieving Continuity of Change in Higher Education (927)
   Barbara K. Curry

8. Crossing Pedagogical Oceans: International Teaching Assistants in U.S. Undergraduate Education (928)
   Rosslyn M. Smith, Patricia Byrd, Gayle L. Nelson, Ralph Pat Barrett, and Janet C. Constantinides

ORDER FORM

Quantity   **Amount**

_____ Please begin my subscription to the current year's *ASHE-ERIC Higher Education Reports* (Volume 25) at $120.00, over 33% off the cover price, starting with Report 1.   _____

_____ Please send a complete set of Volume ____ *ASHE-ERIC Higher Education Reports* at $120.00, over 33% off the cover price.   _____

Individual reports are available for $24.00 and include the cost of shipping and handling.

SHIPPING POLICY:
- Books are sent UPS Ground or equivalent. For faster delivery, call for charges.
- Alaska, Hawaii, U.S. Territories, and Foreign Countries, please call for shipping information.
- Order will be shipped within 24 hours after receipt of request.
- Orders of 10 or more books, call for shipping information.

All prices shown are subject to change.

Returns: No cash refunds—credit will be applied to future orders.

PLEASE SEND ME THE FOLLOWING REPORTS:

Quantity	Volume/No.	Title	Amount

Please check one of the following:
- ☐ Check enclosed, payable to GWU-ERIC.
- ☐ Purchase order attached.
- ☐ Charge my credit card indicated below:
  - ☐ Visa   ☐ MasterCard

Subtotal:	
Less Discount:	
Total Due:	

☐☐☐☐☐☐☐☐☐☐☐☐☐☐☐☐

Expiration Date_____

Name_____

Title_____

Institution _____

Address_____

City _____ State _____ Zip_____

Phone _____ Fax _____ Telex_____

Signature _____ Date_____

SEND ALL ORDERS TO: ASHE-ERIC Higher Education Reports
The George Washington University
One Dupont Cir., Ste. 630, Washington, DC 20036-1183
Phone: (202) 296-2597 • Toll-free: 800-773-ERIC
FAX: (202) 452-1844
http://www.gwu.edu/~eriche